THE REAL PRICE OF FI$

Aberdeen Steam Trawler Losses
1887-1961

by

George F. Ritchie

HUTTON PRESS
1991

Published by the Hutton Press Ltd.
130 Canada Drive, Cherry Burton, Beverley
North Humberside, HU17 7SB

Printed and bound by

Clifford Ward & Co. (Bridlington) Ltd.,
55 West Street, Bridlington, East Yorkshire,
YO15 3DZ

ISBN 1 872167 19 5

DEDICATION

This book is dedicated to all those who sailed on

Aberdeen's steam trawlers, in peace and war, especially

to those who lost their lives and to the families who

awaited their return.

CONTENTS

ACKNOWLEDGEMENTS

I would like to record my gratitude to the following persons for their kind assistance, co-operation and encouragement in the preparation of this book:-

To the Chief Librarian, H.M. Customs & Excise for permission to research the Fishing Boat and Shipping Registers at Aberdeen and to the local Registrars, Mrs Carole Crowther and Mrs Anne Wilson for their help.

To the Head Librarian, Aberdeen City Libraries and the staffs of the Central and Woodside libraries for assistance in the research of old newspapers.

To Roy Leach for recording for me information from the Merchant Navy & Fishing Fleets War Memorial, London and records at Lloyds Register of Shipping.

To Tommy Watt and Ian Tait of the Shetland Museum for allowing me to examine some of their records and for providing photographs.

To my former shipmate Jim Robertson of North Roe for arranging contacts in Shetland.

To George P. Wiseman, a valued friend from my schooldays in Aberdeen, for the painting on the cover.

To the following for photographs supplied:-

George Coull, John Edwards, Arthur Robertson, George Leiper, David Craig, Alex Bruce, George Bruce, Albert Runcie, Ian Nicolson, Robert Johnson, Robert Wiseman, Angus MacLeod, Douglas Gove, Ian Hughson, Mrs. Anna Watt.

To Brenda Aitchison for so willingly and expeditiously typing the text from my almost illegible handwriting.

To my wife Dorothy for her help and encouragement over many years.

George Ritchie,
Stonehaven,
January 1991.

INTRODUCTION

Prior to the introduction of steam trawling in 1882 the city of Aberdeen was relatively unimportant as a fishing centre. A number of line-fishing boats operated from the district of Footdee, at the harbour mouth, supplying the local retail outlets, and the supply was augmented by the catches of fishermen working from tiny harbours and inlets along the coast. Trawling had been the chief method of fishing at English ports, employing sailing trawlers which used a beam trawl, i.e. the mouth of the net was held open by a wooden beam up to 60 ft long. The propulsion of the vessel, and thus also the method of fishing, was entirely dependent on the wind. A North Shields owner named Purdy, who had used steam tugs to tow his sailing trawlers when they were becalmed, hit on the idea of operating the fishing gear from the tug itself, and so the first steam trawler was in use at North Shields in 1877.

A syndicate of eleven Aberdeen businessmen purchased the *Toiler*, a steam tug from Dublin, early in 1882 and commenced fishing with her from Aberdeen in March 1882 amid a storm of controversy, particularly from the fishermen of Footdee, who felt that their livelihood was being taken from them. Within a few months, however, the *Toiler* had proved so successful that her shareholders had recouped their outlay and other owners, including several of the Footdee fishermen, were encouraged to invest in the industry. By 1890 ten steam trawlers were registered in Aberdeen and several others were based there, although they were registered at other ports, especially North and South Shields. By this time, too, fishermen from the smaller towns and villages around the north-east coast were flocking to Aberdeen in search of more steady and rewarding work. Not only fishermen were attracted to

Aberdeen for the new industry; there was also a need for men with experience of steam engines and these were recruited in considerable numbers from country districts, where steam traction engines had been in use for many years. Many successful English trawl skippers were attracted to Aberdeen, and several went on to own their own vessels and later to establish companies which were to become well-known names in the industry.

By 1891, 65 steam trawlers and liners were registered in Aberdeen, by 1905 the numbers had increased to 204 and by 1914 to 294. The outbreak of war in 1914 led to the requisitioning of no less than 228 trawlers and 15 drifters registered in Aberdeen. 36 of Aberdeen's fleet were lost on Naval service, while 42 fishing trawlers were sunk by U-boats and five were mined. To try to compensate for some of these losses Aberdeen owners were obliged to buy some 70 steam vessels of various kinds, mainly from English ports, and convert them for fishing. Most of those that survived the war were scrapped soon afterwards as more suitable replacements in the shape of Admiralty-built trawlers became available after their war service was complete.

Thirteen ex-German trawlers which had been captured and used for Naval service during the war, including two which had been seized at Aberdeen Fish Market on 4th August 1914, were bought by Aberdeen owners, and a further five German trawlers built during the war were brought to Aberdeen in 1922 by the Walker Steam Trawl Fishing Co. Ltd and given 'Star' names, but all five were sold back to Germany in 1923. During the inter-war period the number of trawlers registered in Aberdeen remained fairly steady at around 300, but conditions in the industry deteriorated considerably in comparison with the position prior to 1914. Only 40 new trawlers were built for Aberdeen owners in the 1920's and 1930's, although 88 trawlers had been lost at sea in that period and a considerable number had gone for scrap.

As in 1914, the Admiralty made heavy demands on the fishing fleets as soon as war broke out again in 1939, as it was impossible for the minesweeping capacity of the

S.S. St. Clair – *The Aberdeen – Lerwick mail steamer* **St. Clair** *(1637 tons/1937) is struck by a lump of sea while battling to round the South Breakwater at the entrance to Aberdeen Harbour in a south-east gale. This dramatic picture illustrates vividly the conditions faced frequently during winter by Aberdeen's trawlermen. The trawler* **Empress** *was lost with all her crew at this spot on 23 December 1915. (Photo North Roe Photographic Club).*

Royal Navy, which amounted to only 42 Fleet minesweepers (23 of them from World War I) and 55 minesweeping trawlers, to try to keep ports, anchorages and convoy channels clear of mines. Within a few months, only a relatively small number of trawlers were left in Aberdeen to carry on fishing, and even the few that were left were soon being attacked mercilessly by the German Luftwaffe, in spite of the fact that they were not being used for any military purpose and initially were completely undefended. No less than 17 Aberdeen registered trawlers were lost by air attack and 7 fell victim to mines, while others were seriously damaged by machine-gun fire, several on more than one occasion.

By the time peace returned and those trawlers which had been taken up by the Admiralty were released and converted back to fishing, Aberdeen's fleet was depleted not only by its wartime losses but also by the sale of many of its more modern trawlers to other ports. Only four steam trawlers were built for Aberdeen owners immediately after the war and the fact that a high proportion of the fleet had, by virtue of age, become uneconomic to run and had gone for scrap meant that by 1950 less than 200 steam trawlers remained in Aberdeen, over 100 less than at the outbreak of war. Over the next ten years, the steam trawler was steadily replaced by the motor trawler, the first of which, the *Star of Scotland*, was built for the Walker Company in 1947. By 1960 almost all of Aberdeen's pre-war fleet of steam trawlers had gone, and the last one of all the *Avondow*, built in 1946, went to the scrapyard in February 1967, exactly 85 years after the arrival in Aberdeen of the *Toiler*, the city's first steam trawler.

In those 85 years, fishing had become the most important industry in Aberdeen, providing employment not only to several thousand fishermen in the city itself and from the towns and villages as far away as Buckie on the Moray Firth coast, but also to all the ancillary industries such as fish processing, transport, ice, net and basket-making, coaling, provisioning, engineering, repairing and shipbuilding. Aberdeen itself had expanded considerably to provide the housing required by the large number of families drawn to the city to support the industry, and the suburb of Torry, on the south bank of the River Dee, had become the fishing quarter of the city. It is remarkable how many of the fishermen whose names appear in this book had addresses in Torry, mostly in Victoria Road.

During the 85-year reign of the steam trawler, over 1500 had been registered in Aberdeen and over 300 ships had been lost at sea by various causes. It is clear that these losses had a serious effect on the families whose lives depended on these ships, whether by the loss of life of the family breadwinner or the loss of employment. It is primarily for the families of these men who lost their lives on Aberdeen trawlers that I have set out in this book the details of all of Aberdeen's steam trawler losses, with as much detail of the circumstances of each loss as I have been able to discover. Where lives were lost, I have endeavoured to record the names and home addresses of the victims, but I must make it clear that in many cases no details have been published, especially during wartime when a strict censorship was enforced. I should also make it clear that, with only a few exceptions, what I have recorded are the losses of ships actually registered in Aberdeen, whether or not they were based in Aberdeen at the time; I have not recorded the losses of Aberdeen-based ships registered at other ports, nor instances where a trawler was stranded but later salvaged and returned to service.

Where more than one ship of the same name has been lost I have used the symbols (1) and (2) to distinguish them in the text of this book, but I must emphasise that these symbols were not part of the vessel's name. The figures following the vessel's name in the text show the ship's fishing registration number, the gross registered tonnage and the year of build.

Where all or some of the crew were rescued I have tried to record the means of rescue with the names of rescuers where possible. It is quite remarkable to notice, especially in the earlier years, how many men owed their lives to the life-saving apparatus crews, most of whom were part-time volunteers, particularly around the coast from Fraserburgh to Aberdeen and also in Orkney and Shetland. The main reason for the high incidence of this type of rescue would seem to be that, in the days before echo sounders and radar, navigation in stormy conditions and poor visibility was far from easy, and with a crew, weary after a week's hard fishing, searching in vain for a landmark on the low-lying parts of the Aberdeenshire coast, it was not surprising that the first indication of land was when the keel grounded on the sandy coast. In many cases sea conditions ruled out the possibility of a rescue by lifeboat, if indeed a lifeboat was stationed within reach at the time, so that the only means of rescue available was the rocket apparatus.

The contribution of Aberdeen's trawlermen to the prosperity of the city and of the North-East of Scotland in peacetime and to the service of their country in wartime by Naval service or by the provision of food for the nation should never be under-estimated. We owe them an immense debt of gratitude and I hope that this book will go some way towards repaying that debt.

George Ritchie

ABERDEEN STEAM TRAWLER LOSSES

31 March 1887 *Toiler* A 50   118 Tons/1868

The *Toiler* was the first steam trawler to be registered in Aberdeen, having been bought from Dublin, where she had been employed as a paddle-driven tug, in March 1882 by a syndicate of eleven Aberdeen businessmen. She left Aberdeen on her last trip on the night of 28th March, but had to call in at Fraserburgh next morning on account of rough weather and sheltered there for the rest of the day. On putting to sea again, all went well until she was just off the Orkney Isles, when a gale sprang up and increased in strength until the *Toiler's* deck was being swept from stem to stern by heavy waves. The trawler's pumps were brought into use to prevent her hold being flooded, but waves continually breaking over the vessel extinguished the boiler fires and the ship became unmanageable. While driving before the wind, a tremendous wave carried the mast overboard and the crew gave up all hope of saving their ship. At this stage a steamer was sighted and a flag was hoisted on the *Toiler's* funnel, but this failed to attract the attention of the distant vessel. A fishing boat was next hailed, and this vessel hove to and lay in the vicinity of the disabled *Toiler* for about two hours, until it was thought that the *Toiler* would be able to reach a place of safety, and the fishing boat continued on its course. The condition of the *Toiler*, however, became more precarious, and when another trawler hove in sight distress flares were lit to attract her attention. This turned out to be the trawler *Royal Duke*, owned in Aberdeen and registered in North Shields, which immediately bore down on the *Toiler* and pulled to safety her seven-man crew, all of whom were now in a state of exhaustion. The crew were unable to save any of their effects, and the *Toiler* soon afterwards went down, some distance off the east coast of Caithness. Skipper Henry Denham of the *Royal Duke* was later presented with a pair of binoculars by the Board of Trade for his timely rescue of the crew.

April 1887 *Palmerston* A 328   97 Tons/1866

Like the *Toiler*, the *Palmerston* was a converted tug, driven by paddles, and carried a crew of seven. While fishing in the Moray Firth, 15 miles from Lossiemouth, she sprang a leak underneath her boiler and foundered in a short time. Her crew were able to launch their own smallboat and were picked up by the trawler *J.P. Reynoldson* of South Shields (SSS 269) and taken to Aberdeen.

17 November 1893 *North Sea* A 245   120 Tons/1888

The *North Sea* was the first of 13 screw-driven steam trawlers built for William Pyper in Aberdeen yards between 1888 and 1894. She carried a crew of seven, and left Aberdeen for a fishing trip on 17 November 1893. She was never seen again, and was presumed to have been overwhelmed in a storm about the 20th November.

9 April 1894 *Fastnet* A 422   83 Tons

The *Fastnet* was a small trawler bought second-hand from Cardiff in 1890. She is recorded as having sunk off the island of Gigha, Argyll, but no further details can be found.

21 December 1894 *North East* A473   123 Tons/1890

The *North East*, another William Pyper trawler built by Hall Russell's, had been missing since leaving Aberdeen on 21 December 1894, with her crew of eight for a fishing trip to the Fisher bank, 180 miles N.E. of Aberdeen. She had sufficient coal for three weeks and was due back by 1st January. The two engineers were a father and son from Old Aberdeen.

20 December 1894 *Bonito* A 93   78 Tons/1882

The *Bonito*, a screw-driven ex Thames tug converted for trawling, was driven ashore in a gale a mile north of the mouth of the River Ythan, near Newburgh. Her crew of seven were rescued by Newburgh lifeboat. The crew later reboarded the trawler to attempt to refloat her with the assistance of the tug *Fairweather* from Aberdeen, but the wind increased considerably and the crew had to be rescued for a second time, this time by Collieston Life Saving Apparatus.

12 November 1896   *Craig-Gowan*   A 779

112 Tons/1896

The *Craig-Gowan* was a steam line-fishing vessel completed by Hall Russell's only ten months previously in January 1896. She ran ashore near Scotstoun Head, north of Peterhead, in fog, and her crew were rescued by Peterhead Lifeboat.

27 October 1899   *Dewdrop*   A 11   70 Tons/1883

The *Dewdrop* was a wooden steam line-fishing vessel with a crew of eight. She was Anstruther-built and purchased second-hand from Dundee only months earlier. She ran ashore on a skerry named the Swarf at Rothiesholm, Stronsay, Orkney. The skipper, James Mutch, 59 Menzies Road, Aberdeen, and four of his crew went ashore in Stronsay in the ship's smallboat to seek assistance, and walked the four miles to the local post office to telegraph the owner in Aberdeen. On their return to their boat they found that a severe westerly gale had got up, the sea was by then driving right over the *Dewdrop* and they were unable to re-launch the smallboat to rescue the three crew members who were still on board. The three men made a raft from deck fittings and launched themselves from the ship, but two of them were drowned and it was about three hours before the only survivor of the three, the ship's mate, John Robertson, 42 Walker Road, Aberdeen, got ashore and sought assistance at a nearby farm. The *Dewdrop* was carried over the skerry by the sea and sank, but she was later salvaged and became the Wick drifter *Acacia*(WK 561).

6 February 1900   *Tento*   A 90   148 Tons/1899

The *Tento* was a brand-new trawler completed only in October 1899 by Alexander Hall & Co. for William Slater & Sons, Fishcurers, Albert Quay, Aberdeen. She left Aberdeen on 6th February for a twelve day trip and was never seen again. Skipper Alex. Slater, a single man of 31, had written to his father in Lossiemouth to tell him that he might try his luck at Shetland on this trip. On 26th February a farmer near Fraserburgh picked up a bottle from the beach containing what purported to be a message from the *Tento* saying she was disabled 50 miles from Kinnaird Head and requested immediate assistance. This was thought to be a hoax, until a lifebelt from the trawler was washed up three days later less than ten miles away. The message was undated and unsigned, but it was thought that the writing was similar to that of the second engineer. The ship's bell is now in the possession of a great-grandson of the trawler's owner, but no details of how this was discovered have been traced and it can only be assumed that the bell, having been fixed to the wooden wheelhouse, would have come free as the wood disintegrated, and may have been trawled up by another vessel, as happened with the bell of the *Countess* which was lost in 1901.

The *Tento*'s crew were:

Skipper: Alex Slater (31), 12 Walker Road — Single
Mate: Alex Slater (40), (cousin of skipper) 12 Menzies Road — Family of six
Sec. Fish.: Alex Gerard (30), 10 Seaton Place — Family of one
Ch. Eng.: Charles Black, Footdee — Family of seven
Sec. Eng.: George Simpson, 17 James Street — Family of four
Deckhand: John McLennan, Walker Road — Family of two
Deckhand: Robert Fraser (38), 4 Garvock Street — Family of one
Fireman: Charles McDonald, 24 Water Lane — Family of two
Cook: Wilson, 13 Harvey Place, Banff — Family of six

Strathtay – The Builder's Plate from the Strathtay (A 661), recovered by a diver near Sumburgh Head in 1977. The Strathtay had been missing since leaving Aberdeen on 9 February 1900, and the recovery of this plate, now in the Shetland Museum, finally identified the trawler, which had been seen in difficulties near Sumburgh in a severe storm on 16th February 1900.
(Photo Shetland Museum).

9 February 1900   *Strathtay*   A 661   155 Tons/1891

The *Strathtay* was the third trawler to be built for the fleet of the Aberdeen Steam Trawling and Fishing Co. Ltd. owned by Aberdeen businessman John Brown, a fleet that was to have over sixty trawlers built for it. The *Strathtay* left Aberdeen on 9th February with nine of a crew and was never heard of again. In 1977, wreckage washed ashore near Sumburgh Shetland included the builder's plate from the *Strathtay*; it is believed that she was wrecked on Horse Island near Sumburgh during the storm of 16th February 1900, as a trawler was seen near Horse Island from Sumburgh Head lighthouse steaming to her anchors in the storm. Her lights came on as dusk fell and distress flares were seen later. However, no means of rescue was available and the trawler had been overwhelmed in that most dangerous place.

16 February 1900   *Ben Nevis*   A 821   124 Tons/1897

The *Ben Nevis* owned by the North British Steam Fishing Co. Ltd, was yet another victim of the great storm of 16th February 1900. She was swept ashore at Kirkton Head, St Fergus and all eight members of her crew were lost, three of whom were from Aberdeen and the others from Yarmouth.

22 January 1901   *Countess*   A 642   113 Tons/1891

The *Countess*, built in South Shields and owned by Thos. Davidson, sank after collision with S.T. *Strathbran* (A 137) 25 miles north-east of Aberdeen. Her crew were rescued by the *Strathbran*. Ironically, the *Countess's* ship's bell was trawled up in April 1905 by the *Strathdon*, a sister of the *Strathbran*, and handed back to the owners via the Customs authorities.

23 March 1901 *Glengairn*   A 203   64 Tons/1900

The *Glengairn* was a new drifter belonging to the Steam Herring Fleet Ltd of Aberdeen. Fire broke out aboard the vessel (a wooden one) and quickly got out of hand. The crew were able to get away in their own smallboat and the ship sank 2 miles from the island of Horse of Copinsay, Orkney.

6 November 1902 *Prestige*   A 793   131 Tons/1896

The *Prestige*, belonging to W.H. Dodds of Aberdeen, ran ashore on Cairnbulg Brigg and her crew of nine were rescued by the local life saving apparatus.

25 December 1902   *Ocean Racer*
                                    A 671   155 Tons/1892

The *Ocean Racer* was a small steam trawler 100 feet long built at Glasgow in 1892 and owned by Meff Brothers, Commercial Quay, Aberdeen. On 16th December 1902, with a crew of nine and under the command of Skipper Richard Fox, 25 Urquhart Road, Aberdeen, she was trawling 150 miles north-east of Buchan Ness. In the early morning a strong south-easterly gale got up, which compelled the crew to haul up their gear and secure everything on deck to ride out the storm. At 9 a.m. that day the boiler failed, leaving them entirely at the mercy of the sea, and they began to fear that they might be driven on to a lee shore on the Shetland Islands. During the afternoon the wind backed into the north and increased to hurricane force. At six o'clock a trawler hove in sight and the *Ocean Racer* ran up a flag requesting assistance, but no notice was taken of it.

Next day the weather moderated somewhat, and at 2 p.m. another trawler was sighted, but again no notice was taken of the plight of the *Ocean Racer* in spite of her distress flag. That night the lights of two more trawlers were sighted but the *Ocean Racer* was unable to attract their attention.

During the following three days, the tiny trawler continued to be battered by huge waves and the wind was again blowing a hurricane. By now the crew's food supplies were almost exhausted, so they rationed themselves to one biscuit a day and some salt fish. On the afternoon of Christmas Day, the wind was still at hurricane force and the sleet and snow accompanying it were so thick that visibility was almost nil. Suddenly, a lighthouse was sighted and the anchor was put down with its full length of chain to try to prevent the trawler from driving ashore. The anchor could not hold, however, and as it was inevitable that the ship would be driven ashore, fires were lit on deck to summon assistance. At nine o'clock in the evening the *Ocean Racer* finally grounded near the town of Stavanger in Norway. As the seas were now breaking over her, the crew took to the rigging.

A local life-saving apparatus arrived very promptly and immediately succeeded in firing a line over the ship. As the ship's hull was by now under water, the crew had great difficulty in retrieving the line and making it fast to the rigging, but at 10 p.m. the first man was hauled ashore in the breeches buoy. The rescue appears to have been prolonged, probably on account of the severe weather, and it was early on Boxing Day before Skipper Fox got safely to dry land. The local farmers sheltered the exhausted crew, providing them with warm food and dry clothing until they could be shipped home from Stavanger to Hull, and thence to Aberdeen via Newcastle.

4 September 1903 *Belcher*   A 341   148 Tons/1893

The *Belcher* was a Hall Russell built trawler, completed for South Shields owners and registered SSS 15 until being bought by Peter Johnstone with her sister *Bendigo* SSS 13 (later A 338) in April 1901. The *Belcher* ran ashore on the morning of 4th September 1903, a half mile north of Collieston. The crew were landed safely, presumably by life saving apparatus although no details were given. The Mate appeared at Aberdeen Sheriff Court only five days later charged with negligent seamanship. The wreck was sold for £3 5s 0d to a Leeds salvage firm who had men working on a wreck at Cruden Bay.

9 February 1904   *Campania* (1)   A 486
149 Tons/1901

The *Campania*, a Tyne built trawler formerly SN 282 and owned by the Eastern Steam Fishing Co. Ltd since November 1901, foundered in the entrance channel of Aberdeen Harbour after being driven against the North Pier while entering the harbour in a severe south-easterly gale. All nine crew were promptly rescued by the Aberdeen pulling and sailing lifeboat. A graphic description of the rescue is given in J.R. Duthie's book *To the Rescue*.

(A second *Campania* A 437 was lost by U-Boat action on 26th June 1915).

21 March 1904   *Ibis*   A 61   142 Tons/1892

The *Ibis* stranded on the Rumble Rocks in Yell Sound, Shetland, in a heavy snowstorm. Her crew were rescued by the Aberdeen trawler *Sunbeam* A 680, which herself was lost on 31st October the following year at Borwick Head, Sanday, Orkney. The *Ibis* and four of her sisters, *Brent*, *Coot*, *Eider* and *Grebe*, all built in Port Glasgow in 1892, were brought to Aberdeen in 1899 by the Silver City Steam Trawling Co. Ltd. *Ibis* was sold to Peter Johnstone in 1902.

6 April 1904   *Ben Venue*   A 83   151 Tons/1899

The *Ben Venue* was built by Hall Russell's for the North British Steam Fishing Co. Ltd. She stranded on the Skerry Rock off Boddam but succeeded in refloating herself, only to founder shortly afterwards. Her crew of nine got safely away in their smallboat and were picked up by the Grimsby trawler *Baltic* (GY 186).

16 January 1905   *Banffshire*   A 349   213 Tons/1901

The *Banffshire*, built by Mackie & Thomson of Govan for the Shire Steam Fishing Co. Ltd. sailed from Aberdeen on 12th January 1905 for an Iceland fishing trip under Skipper Alfred Jones, 158 Victoria Road, and his crew of ten. On 16th January she ran ashore in heavy weather on the south-west coast of Iceland on the east side of Reidaross. Just before grounding, her smallboat had been smashed to pieces and washed overboard, so that the crew had to wait for 28 hours before the sea calmed sufficiently to allow them to get ashore by wading through the chest-high water towards the distant beach of black sand. In the words of a newspaper report at the time "they seemed to have struck a nasty place in which to pile a vessel up". The point where they had come ashore was on the bank of a river which had to be forded to get to the nearest habitation in a very sparsely populated district. The river was in full flood, making crossing impossible in the torrent of broken ice and water which poured down. To make matters worse, there were streams on each side of them, and in their dejected condition, with sodden clothing in a temperature of five degrees below zero and in almost continuous darkness at that time of year, the eleven men huddled together behind a rock to shelter from the biting wind. In the freezing conditions, it is questionable whether any of the men would have survived till morning had not an Icelandic farmer, Bjorn Paulsen, been on the outlook for wreckage being washed ashore after the storm. He spotted the wreck of the *Banffshire* and, coming to get a closer view, it did not take him long to find that there was no-one on board. He then spotted the footprints of the crew in the soft sand, and came on the castaways behind the rock. He at once set about the task of getting the men to safety with the least possible delay, and took each of them over the river on his one pony before conveying them to his lonely farmhouse. As there was not sufficient room to accommodate a further eleven guests, Paulsen turned out his farm animals from the byre to make room for the men. They had to stay at the farm for eight days till 24th January, when, with the assistance of seven guides and with a sheriff's assistant as interpreter, they set out in severe weather on the long journey to Reykjavik. This took them thirteen days, mainly on horseback, and they spent each night at isolated farms where they were invariably entertained most hospitably. At last, on the

6th February, they reached Reykjavik in a state of weariness and exhaustion, and had to wait a further four days before joining the mail steamer *Laura* on her regular sailing to Leith, which they reached on 14th February, thirty-four days after leaving their homes in Aberdeen.

21 March 1905   *Loch Tay*   A 888   197 Tons/1903

Built by Duthie's for the Bon Accord Steam Fishing Co. Ltd. the *Loch Tay* stranded in fog near Rattray Head. The crew of ten were able to leave the ship in their own boat.

14 April 1905   *Star of the East*   A 565   208 Tons/1902

Wrecked near East London, South Africa, the *Star of the East* had been built by Smiths Dock, North Shields as the *Snowdrop* for the Union Steam Fishing Co. Ltd. of Aberdeen and had been re-named in 1904.

1 September 1905   *Swallow*   A 112   134 Tons/1893

The *Swallow*, a small steam liner, was wrecked on Sealskerry, at the Northern tip of North Ronaldsay, Orkney. Her crew of nine were saved. The Aberdeen trawler *St. Nicholas* (A 489) was lost at the same spot on 4th November 1912.

26 September 1905   *Kate*   A 736   93 Tons/1893

The *Kate*, a small trawler built by Marrs of Leith for John Lewis, foundered off the Spurn Light, at the entrance to the Humber, after a collision with the North Shields drifter *Redvers Buller* (SN 297), which rescued the crew and landed them at Grimsby.

31 October 1905   *Sunbeam*   A 680   166 Tons/1892

The *Sunbeam*, built by Duthies for Johnston & Sherrit of Aberdeen, was wrecked at Borwick Head, Sanday, Orkney in a gale. Two of her crew, the mate and the second engineer, managed to climb a 100ft crag and haul their shipmates to safety by ladder and ropes. *Sunbeam*

had saved the crew of the Aberdeen trawler *Ibis* (A 61) when she was wrecked in Yell Sound, Shetland on 21st March 1904.

22 January 1906   *Redcap*   A 526   135 Tons/1895

The *Redcap* was a former Grimsby trawler GY 4 built by Earle's of Hull and brought to Aberdeen in 1902 by the Dee Steam Fishing Co. Ltd. She was wrecked at Red Head, Eday, Orkney. Her crew were saved.

25 May 1906   *Glenlossie*   A 205   60 Tons/1900

Glenlossie, a small drifter belonging to the Steam Herring Fleet Ltd, a publicly-quoted Aberdeen company all of whose vessels were named after glens, was sunk in collision with the Wick steam drifter *Fidelia* (WK 563), 13 miles west of Downings Bay, County Donegal, Ireland. Her crew were rescued by the *Fidelia*.

26 May 1906   *Badger*   A 877   200 Tons/1903

Badger was one of the two trawlers built by Scott of Kinghorn Ltd. for the North Sea Steam Co. Ltd. of 20 Adelphi, Aberdeen, her sister being *Bedouin* (A 601). The *Badger* was on her way to Aberdeen after a twelve day fishing trip to Iceland when she stranded on the Bow Rocks at Aikerness, Westray, Orkney, in a dense fog. The Westray life saving apparatus could not approach closely enough to fire a line over the trawler, so they mounted their gear in a small yawl and succeeded in saving all but one of the trawler's crew. The crew member who was lost was the mate, Efa Mortlock of 28 St. Clement Street, who left a widow and six children.

18 January 1907   *Star of the Isles*   A 561   197 Tons/1902

Built by Alexander Hall & Sons for the then rapidly expanding Walker Steam Trawl Fishing Co. Ltd. the *Star of the Isles* was wrecked on the Cruden Scaurs, off Whinnyfold, Aberdeenshire. The crew got safely off in their own boat and landed at Cruden Bay.

29 May 1907   *Marec*   **A 148   182 Tons/1900**

Owned by the Silver City Steam Trawling Co. Ltd. *Marec* was wrecked on the Havdegrind Rocks, a skerry three miles east of the island of Foula, Shetland. The crew got away in their own boat and landed on Foula, from where they were rowed the twenty miles to Scalloway in Shetland in a Foula sixareen, a six-oared rowing boat.

11 September 1907   *Strathbeg*   **A 90   202 Tons/1906**

The trawler *Strathbeg* was one of the growing Strath fleet of trawlers of the Aberdeen Steam Trawling & Fishing Co. Ltd. and was only a year old, having been completed in August 1906. She was first in distress when she stranded at Scotstoun Head, St. Fergus on 18th January 1907. She was refloated and returned to service, but less than eight months later on 11th September she grounded at the Fless, Fair Isle in fog and became a total wreck. Her crew of nine took to their smallboat and stood off until they were guided ashore by islanders.

9 September 1908   *Ben Dearg*   **A 566   209 Tons/1902**

The *Ben Dearg* had been completed by Smiths Dock, North Shields as the *Corinthia* for the Eastern Steam Fishing Co. Ltd. She was sold to the North British Steam Fishing Co. Ltd. in 1906 and re-named *Ben Dearg*. She was wrecked in a storm one mile east of Pennan on the Moray Firth coast. Her skipper, W. Larne, was drowned but the eight other members, including the skipper's brother who was mate, were able to swim or wade over the rocks to safety.

4 December 1908   *Ben Wyvis*   **A 301   159 Tons/1900**

The *Ben Wyvis*, owned by Richard Irvin & Sons Ltd, ran ashore in fog on the rocks two miles north of Collieston on the Aberdeenshire coast. Her crew were rescued by the Collieston life saving apparatus.

5 January 1909   *Lochnagar*   **A 292   165 Tons/1900**

The *Lochnagar*, built by Alexander Hall & Sons and owned by the Loch Line Steam Trawling & Fishing Co.

Ltd, was sunk in collision off Buchan Ness with the steamship *Margaret* of Wick. Her crew of nine were picked up by the *Margaret* and landed in Aberdeen.

11 April 1909   *John Nutten*   **A 846   161 Tons/1898**

The *John Nutten*, owned by the Aberdeen Steam Trawling & Fishing Co Ltd, became fast on an outlying rock south of Fair Isle in hazy weather. She managed to free herself, but smashed her rudder in the attempt, and shortly afterwards began to settle low in the water. The Aberdeen trawler *Ben Aden* (A 303) hove in sight, and in response to her distress signals, she closed the *John Nutten* and took her in tow. After towing for some time, it was clear that the *John Nutten* was unlikely to stay afloat for much longer, so her crew were transferred to the *Ben Aden* and she sank shortly afterwards. The *Ben Aden* brought her crew home to Aberdeen. It was reported in the Aberdeen Daily Journal of 13th April 1909 that "as the crew of the *John Nutten* are all resident in Aberdeen they were in no way inconvenienced, except for the loss of personal belongings."

25 September 1909   *Merlin*   **A 44   129 Tons/1899**

The *Merlin*, a small steam liner owned by W.H. Dodds of Aberdeen, stranded in fog on Red Head, Eday, Orkney. Her crew were saved, but the trawler was a total loss. She was formerly a Grimsby trawler GY 7 and by a strange coincidence was lost at the same spot as *Redcap* (A 526) (also a former Grimsby trawler) was lost on 22nd January 1906.

15 October 1909   *Glenbervie*   **A 364   65 Tons/1901**

The *Glenbervie* was one of the early steam drifters owned by the Steam Herring Fleet Ltd, and was prosecuting the East Anglian Herring fishing when she foundered twelve miles from the Corton Light Vessel, after springing a leak in a westerly gale. Her crew of nine were picked up by the steam drifter *Rose* (INS 285) of Nairn after two trips in their own smallboat.

26 October 1909   *William Osten*   A 856
       113 Tons/1889

The *William Osten*, formerly of North Shields (SN 66) and owned by Johnston & Sherrit, was entering Aberdeen harbour in a northerly gale when her steering gear broke and she was driven on to the rocks between the two breakwaters on the south side of the entrance channel. Her crew were rescued by the Aberdeen Lifeboat but the *William Osten* became a total loss.

20 December 1909   *Ben Roy*   A 94   220 Tons/1906

The *Ben Roy*, owned by Richard Irvin & Sons Ltd, was wrecked near Peniche, on the coast of Portugal. The skipper and the chief engineer were Aberdeen men, while the rest of the crew, one of whom was lost, were Portuguese.

8 March 1910   *Mormond*   A 293   173 Tons/1898

The *Mormond* was one of a dozen trawlers built in Aberdeen and Montrose for the Fraserburgh Steam Trawling Co. Ltd. and named after districts and estates in the Fraserburgh area. She had been bought by Andrew Walker, trawlowner, Aberdeen in 1909 and employed as a steam liner. She ran ashore near Duncansby Head, Caithness on 8th March 1910. Her crew landed safely, but no details of their means of rescue can be traced.

5 April 1910   *Jessie Wetherly*   A 228   215 Tons/1908

The *Jessie Wetherly*, built by Hall Russell's and owned by the Wetherly Steam Fishing Co. Ltd, sank off Iceland after a collision with the French trawler *Nord Caper* (ARC 51) 417 Tons/1907. Her crew of twelve, including Skipper Robert Wetherly, were saved by the French trawler.

21 October 1910   *Aberdeenshire*   A 234
       213 Tons/1900

The *Aberdeenshire*, built at Govan and owned by the Shire Steam Fishing Co. Ltd. grounded on rocks at Craigscaw, Dundonnie, one mile south of Boddam. Her crew of nine were saved by Life Saving Apparatus.

25 November 1910   *Knowsie*   A 306   186 Tons/1899

The *Knowsie*, like the *Mormond*, was an ex-Fraserburgh trawler sold to Aberdeen owners. She stranded at Bursland Bay, Papa Westray, Orkney, and her crew landed without assistance in their own boat.

3 January 1911   *George*   A 345   150 Tons/1893

The small trawler *George* hardly qualifies to be included in a book of Aberdeen trawler losses, as she was registered in Aberdeen on 5th January 1911 and the registration cancelled on the 11th January 1911, with the note that the vessel had been totally lost on 3rd January on Hammonds Knoll. The fishing number A 345 was allocated to her, but she could never have displayed the number and must still have borne her previous number (CF 7) when she was lost.

A newspaper of 4th January 1911 carries the following story:-

ABERDEEN TRAWLER LOST
CREW'S TERRIBLE EXPERIENCE

A graphic story was related at Yarmouth yesterday by the crew of the Cardiff steam trawler *George*, wrecked in the North Sea while on a voyage to Aberdeen, where she was to be employed by her new owner Captain Nicholas Cook.

Skipper Hewitt, of Cardiff, said:- "We left Cardiff on Saturday (31st December 1910) with a crew of six hands, five belonging to Cardiff and George Gill, the chief engineer, of Stafford Street, Aberdeen. We made a fair passage down the Bristol Channel and through the English Channel to Dover, when we encountered a succession of gales. At two o'clock yesterday morning we passed Smith's Knoll Lightship, then shaped a course for the Dudgeon Lightship, but in half an hour the keel of the vessel struck on a sandbank, and the trawler immediately broached to. Heavy seas poured over her aft, driving us all forward. We put out an anchor to bring her into the wind, and we hoisted the mizzen sail, but she would not answer the helm. We got some flares and burned them, while the seas were repeatedly sweeping the deck on which we were hanging for dear life, and we eventually saw rockets shoot up in the sky from some lightship. No help came and the vessel gradually filled. Tons of water poured down into the cabin and the engine room, putting out the fires, and we could see the cabin table floating about. Through the darkness we clung on to the wreck knowing that our vessel must speedily sink, as a faint streak of dawn appeared we got our boat, which was chocked down on the deck, over the side with great difficulty. The third hand, Archie Dupree, a Cardiff man, sustained a terrible wound in the head from a spanging iron block in passing along the deck to get one of our flares.

We saw a gleam of light five miles off and pulled for it, but we an awful passage. It was all we could do to keep her baled. We were four or five hours afloat before we could reach the lightship. A strong current drove us past the lightship, but the lightmen threw a buoy over their stern with a line attached. We picked up the buoy and the lightmen hauled us to their vessel. It proved to be the Wold Lightship, and they treated us very kindly. The Polling lifeboat *Heart of Oak* was out searching for us but could not find us. The Yarmouth tug *King Edward*, which had been searching about since 5 o'clock, having been summoned by wireless, came up, and we left the lightship in our boat. We were taken on board the tug and brought to Yarmouth. The tug went to look for the trawler, but the ship had foundered, and there was no trace left of her."

1 April 1911   *Clan Gordon*   A 902   197 Tons/1903

The Clan Steam Trawling Co. Ltd. commissioned the building of three trawlers in 1903, the *Clan Gordon* (A 902) completed by Hall Russell's in September 1903, and the *Clan Forbes* (A 908) and the *Clan Grant* (A 909), both completed by Smiths Dock Co. Ltd, North Shields in November 1903. The company does not appear to have been very successful, however, as the *Clan Forbes* was sold to Holland in 1910 and the *Clan Grant* to Dublin in 1911. The *Clan Gordon* is recorded at Lloyds as having stranded on Hermit Rock, Inchkeith, Firth of Forth. No

mention of this can be traced in any local newspapers of the time, and as the *Clan Gordon's* registration was not cancelled until 30th December 1911 it is presumed that the crew had been in no danger and that there appeared to be prospects that the ship could be salvaged. In any event, the Clan Steam Trawling Co. Ltd. was wound up in April 1911 — perhaps the loss of the *Clan Gordon* was the last straw.

15 May 1911   *Skomer*   A 194   151 Tons/1896

The *Skomer* was a Duthie-built trawler, bought second-hand from Cardiff in 1907. She was sunk in collision with the Grimsby trawler *Barbados* (GY 71) seven miles ENE of Buchan Ness. Her crew were rescued by the *Barbados* and landed in Aberdeen.

13 October 1911   *Kilrenny*   A 388   97 Tons/1897

The *Kilrenny*, a small steam liner owned by the Inver Steam Line Fishing Co. Ltd, sank after collision in the Humber with the Grimsby trawler *Perseus* (GY 445).

23 December 1911   *Ben More*   A 82   157 Tons/1899

The *Ben More*, owned by Richard Irvin & Sons Ltd, stranded at Whitelink Bay, Inverallochy. Her crew got safely away in their own boat.

19 March 1912   *Strathyre*   A 41   193 Tons/1905

The *Strathyre*, owned by the Aberdeen Steam Trawling & Fishing Co. Ltd, sailed for the fishing grounds on the afternoon of 12th March, but rough weather and tremendous seas were immediately encountered and this persuaded the skipper to return to harbour where, indeed, a great many other vessels were already stormbound. The harbour bar was safely negotiated but there was a heavy swell, with broken seas, and the ship was soon in difficulties, the low water adding to the danger. A large wave lifted the *Strathyre* stern on to the North Pier, about halfway along its length, and there the vessel stuck fast. In view of her closeness to the pier, the Harbourmaster, Captain Crombie, did not call

Braconhill – The wreck of the *Braconhill* after she struck the North Pier at Aberdeen Harbour, following a steering gear failure, on 9 January 1913. Her crew were saved by the local Life-Saving Brigade, but the *Braconhill* became a total loss.
(Photo Aberdeen Museum).

out the lifeboat, but alerted the life saving apparatus. A rope was soon made fast to one of the trawler's masts, and the crew were pulled ashore one by one in the breeches buoy. The *Strathyre* began to break up shortly afterwards and became a total loss.

26 July 1912 *Rob Roy* A 417 149 Tons/1889

The *Rob Roy* collided in dense fog with the Grimsby trawler *Carlton* (GY 270) about twenty miles off Aberdeen. The crew of nine got safely away in their smallboat, just before the *Rob Roy* sank, only ten minutes after the collision. The crew were picked up by the *Carlton* and landed in Aberdeen.

12 August 1912 *Rodney* A 73 112 Tons/1891

The *Rodney* is recorded as having foundered in the Bristol Channel but no further details are available. She was a small trawler purchased from Grimsby in 1906 and

sold to Milford owners in 1909. She retained her Aberdeen registration though she was probably fishing from Milford Haven.

4 November 1912 *St. Nicholas* A 489 207 Tons/1901

The *St. Nicholas*, a Duthie-built ship owned by T. Lauder & G. McLean, was wrecked on the Seal Skerry, North Ronaldsay, Orkney. The Aberdeen trawler *Swallow* had been lost at the same spot on 1st September 1905.

24 December 1912 *St. Andrew* A 670 150 Tons/1892

The *St. Andrew*, owned by Andrew Walker, foundered in gale force winds twelve miles off Strathy Point on the north coast of Caithness. She had been on her way to Aberdeen after landing fish in Glasgow. She ran ashore on Lady Isle, off Troon, and was repaired in Troon but was forced to call in at Stornoway for further repairs on the way. Her crew of seven got away in their smallboat, and after sixteen hours of rowing in tempestuous conditions, they finally succeeded in reaching land five miles west of Strathy.

9 January 1913   *Braconhill*   A 904   194 Tons/1903

The *Braconhill*, built in South Shields and owned by the Don Fishing Co. Ltd, was entering Aberdeen harbour in a south-east gale when her steering gear broke and she was driven against the North Pier, in almost the same spot as the *Strathyre* less than a year earlier. The life-saving apparatus was quickly in position, and the crew were pulled to safety. A description of the wreck is given in J.L. Duthie's book *To the Rescue*.

3 March 1913   *Strathalmond*   A 320   194 Tons/1910

The *Strathalmond*, built by Hall Russell's and owned by the Aberdeen Steam Trawling & Fishing Co. Ltd, sailed from Aberdeen on 3rd March 1913 with her crew of nine, and no further trace of her was ever found.

19 March 1914   *Vale of Endrick*   A 496
214 Tons/1912

The *Vale of Endrick*, built by Duthie's for the Vale of Leven Steam Fishing Co. Ltd, was sunk in collision with the German trawler *Senator Oswald* 179 miles to the north of Aberdeen. Her crew of nine were saved by two boats from the *Senator Oswald*.

27 August 1914   *Crathie* (1)   A 350   210 Tons/1911
***Thomas W. Irvin*   A 421**
201 Tons/1911

These two trawlers had been requisitioned at the start of hostilities on 4th August and were two of a group of four minesweepers based on the Tyne. On 26th August the German minelayer *Albatros* escorted by the cruiser *Stuttgart* laid a field of 194 mines thirty miles east of the Tyne. Within four hours an Icelandic trawler had been blown up, followed shortly afterwards by a Norwegian steamer and a Danish sailing ship. The four sweepers were sent to the scene at 5.30 a.m. next morning as soon as news of the casualties had been received. *Thomas W. Irvin*, with the senior officer of the group on board, was the first to be mined, sinking in less than five minutes with the loss of three of her crew, followed by the *Crathie*, with the loss of two men.

Several trawlers and drifters built during World War I were named after ships which had been lost in the early part of the war. A second *Thomas W. Irvin* (SN 265) of 209 Tons was built in 1915 and served as a minesweeper from February 1916 till 1919. A second *Crathie* (A 713) was built in 1916, but her career was a short one. Taken over as a minesweeper in November 1916, she was wrecked on 16th December 1916 on Nizam Point, Barra Head.

5 October 1914   *Drumoak*   A 516   208 Tons/1902

The *Drumoak*, built by Halls and owned by the North of Scotland Steam Fishing Co. Ltd. was mined and sunk off the Belgian coast while on Naval service.

18 April 1915   *Glencarse*   A 605   188 Tons/1900

The *Glencarse*, a Duthie-built ship owned by William Hutchison, left Aberdeen on 8th April 1915 for a twelve day fishing trip to Faroe waters under Skipper William Wright, 8 Affleck Street, with a crew of eight, all Torry men except one of the fishermen who hailed from Millwall. On 18th April she was within a few miles of her home port when she was stopped by a German U-Boat, a prize crew were put on board and she and her crew were taken to Cuxhaven in Germany. Her crew were interned in Germany for the rest of the war.

27 April 1915   *Balmedie*   A 113   205 Tons/1906

The *Balmedie*, built by Hall Russell's for the Balgownie Steam Trawl Fishing Co. Ltd, had been taken up by the Navy for minesweeping in August 1914. She was sunk in the Dardanelles while on Naval service.

2 May 1915   *Sunray*   A 669   165 Tons/1891

The *Sunray* was a Duthie-built ship owned by A.J. Freeth of North Shields. She was captured by a U-Boat and sunk by gunfire 56 miles NNE of Longstone Light.

2 May 1915   *Martaban*   A 527 ' 148 Tons/1890

The *Martaban* was an iron-built ship bought second-hand from Hull in 1912 by R. & J. Moon, Butchers in Victoria Road, who seemed to specialise in old trawlers. She was captured by a U-Boat and sunk by gunfire 22 miles E by N of Aberdeen. Her crew got away in their smallboat and arrived in Stonehaven after seventeen hours rowing.

2 May 1915   *Cruiser*   GN 54   146 Tons/1898

The *Cruiser* was based in Aberdeen, with an Aberdeen crew. She was sunk by U-Boat gunfire fifty miles SE of Aberdeen. Her Skipper, Alex Palmer, 77 Regent Quay and three crew members were killed, four were wounded and only one was unhurt. The survivors were brought to Aberdeen by the steamer *T.W. Stuart*.

3 May 1915   *Scottish Queen*   A 384   126 Tons/1889

The *Scottish Queen* was one of the earliest Aberdeen trawlers, being built in 1889 by Scotts of Kinghorn for Robert Brown, who is described as a water tacksman of 31 Rubislaw Den South, Aberdeen. She was captured by U-Boat and sunk by gunfire 50 miles ESE of Aberdeen. Her crew of eight were rescued by the Aberdeen trawler *Jane Ross* (A 454), "having been hospitably treated by the Germans", according to a newspaper report.

7 May 1915   *Benington*   A 236   131 Tons/1890

The *Benington* was built of iron in South Shields and was transferred from Peterhead registry only four months previously. She was captured by U-Boat and sunk by gunfire ten miles SE of Peterhead near the Cruden Scaurs. The crew were picked up by a Norwegian vessel and were finally landed at Aberdeen by the trawler *Forth* (A 433).

19 May 1915   *Crimond*   A 334   173 Tons/1899

The *Crimond*, another of the ill-fated ex-Fraserburgh trawlers, was captured by U-Boat and sunk by a bomb planted on board 60 miles east of Wick.

(*Crimond* had gone ashore on 9th February 1912 near the Holms of Eyre, Sanday, Orkney. Four crew members were lost when their smallboat was dashed to pieces, one managed to scramble ashore, and the remaining four were saved by the Stronsay motor lifeboat. The bodies of the crew were brought to Aberdeen by the S.T. *Ben Doran* (A 178), which herself was lost tragically on 29th March 1930. *Crimond* was refloated on 23rd February 1912.)

19 May 1915   *Lucerne*   SD   154 Tons/1896

The *Lucerne*, although registered in Sunderland, was owned by Robert and Joseph Moon, butchers in Aberdeen, and carried an Aberdeen crew under Skipper Frederick Powdrell. While fishing 50 miles NE by N of Rattray Head, the trawler was boarded by a boarding party from a U-Boat and the crew ordered to row across to the U-Boat in their own boat and to line up on deck. Two German officers then got two of the trawler's crew to row them across to the *Lucerne*, where they placed time bombs and also helped themselves to some freshly caught fish. The Germans insisted on paying two marks for the fish taken and put the Aberdeen crew aboard the Danish ship, *Urda*, on a voyage from Dysart to Iceland with coal. The *Urda* landed them in Fraserburgh. The press report concluded:- "The crew took their own kitbags home."

3 June 1915   *Strathbran* (1)   A 137   163 Tons/1899

Built by Hall Russell's for the Aberdeen Steam Trawling & Fishing Co. Ltd. the *Strathbran* was captured by U-Boat and sunk by gunfire 35 ESE of Pentland Skerries.

3 June 1915   *Chrysoprasus*   A 145   119 Tons/1907

Built by Hall Russell's for Torry owner A.W. Ritchie, *Chrysoprasus* was captured by a U-Boat and sunk by gunfire 45 miles E x S of Papa Stronsay, Orkney.

4 June 1915   *Petrel*   A 515   187 Tons/1902

The *Petrel* was a Duthie-built boat owned by the Silver

City Steam Trawling Co. Ltd. She was captured by a U-Boat and sunk by gunfire 55 miles NNE from Buchan Ness.

4 June 1915   *Ebenezer*   A 892   113 Tons/1903

The *Ebenezer* was built by Scotts of Kinghorn and owned by Thomas Davidson. She was captured by a U-Boat and sunk by gunfire 117 miles SW x S from Out Skerries, Shetland.

4 June 1915   *Evening Star* (1)   A 530   120 Tons/1895

The *Evening Star* was captured by a U-Boat and sunk by gunfire 50 miles ESE of Copinsay, Orkney. *Evening Star* was one of two trawlers built by Halls for Thos. Walker, the *Morning Star*, which was sold to France in 1926 and the *Evening Star*, sold to Peterhead in 1899. The *Evening Star* came back to Aberdeen in 1902 under the ownership of Thomas Ritchie, Torry.

4 June 1915   *Cortes*   A 290   174 Tons/1899

A Hall Russell built ship owned by Andrew Walker, the *Cortes* was in company with the *Evening Star* when she was captured by a U-Boat and sunk by a bomb placed on board 50 miles ESE of Copinsay, Orkney.

4 June 1915   *Explorer*   A 535   156 Tons/1894

The *Explorer* was previously a Hull trawler H 245, brought to Aberdeen in 1912 under the joint ownership of H.W. Foulger, Outfitter, 178 Union Grove, and Skipper J.M. Barber, 163 Crown Street. She was captured by a U-Boat and sunk by gunfire 73 miles NE x N of Buchan Ness.

5 June 1915   *Star of the West*   A 548   197 Tons/1902

Built by Halls for the Walker Steam Trawl Fishing Co. Ltd. the *Star of the West* was captured by a U-Boat and sunk by gunfire 55 miles NE of Buchan Ness.

5 June 1915   *Japonica*   A 193   145 Tons/1896

The *Japonica* was bought from Milford Haven only six months earlier by trawlowner R.W. Lewis. She was captured by a U-Boat and sunk by gunfire 45 miles east of Kinnaird Head.

9 June 1915   *Schiehallion*   A 905   198 Tons/1903

The *Schiehallion*, built by Duthies and owned by the Grampian Fishing Co. Ltd. was taken up for minesweeping in August 1914. She was mined and sunk in the Dardanelles while on Naval service. A replacement for her was built by Duthies for the company in 1916 and named *Schiehallion* (A 727).

20 June 1915   *Premier*   A 471   169 Tons/1901

The *Premier*, built by Halls, was purchased from North Shields in 1912 by W.H. Dodds. She was captured by a U-Boat and sunk by gunfire 75 miles N x W of Troup Head.

23 June 1915   *Lebanon*   A 441   111 Tons/1907

The *Lebanon* was built in 1907 for Peterhead owner David D. Noble, who transferred her to Aberdeen registration in 1912. She was captured by a U-Boat and sunk by gunfire 30 miles E x N of Muckle Flugga, Shetland.

23 June 1915   *Viceroy*   A 598   150 Tons/1899

The *Viceroy* was built by Halls and was registered at North Shields SN 10 until being registered in Aberdeen in December 1913 by Skipper A. Brodie. She was captured by a U-Boat and sunk by gunfire 50 miles ENE of Out Skerries, Shetland.

24 June 1915   *Vine*   A 279   110 Tons/1900

The *Vine* had been built by Forbes & Birnie, Peterhead for Aberdeen owner Thomas Davidson. She was captured by a U-Boat and sunk by gunfire 50 miles NE x E of Out Skerries, Shetland.

24 June 1915   *Commander*   A 226   149 Tons/1899

The *Commander* had been built in Leith for Granton owner T. L. Devlin and registered as GN 63. She came to

Aberdeen in 1908, owned by R. Craig of Torry, and was captured by a U-Boat and sunk by gunfire 49 miles E of Baltasound, Shetland.

26 June 1915   *Campania* (2)   A 437   167 Tons/1895

The *Campania* was built in Beverley, and prior to coming to Aberdeen in 1912 was owned by Neale & West of Cardiff (CF 1). Her Aberdeen owners were W. Walker and others. She was captured by a U-Boat and sunk by gunfire 60 miles N x W of Hoy Head. (A previous *Campania* (A 486) was wrecked in the entrance channel of Aberdeen harbour on 9th February 1904.)

6 July 1915   *Strathgarry*   A 97   202 Tons/1906

The *Strathgarry* was built by Hall Russell's and owned by the Aberdeen Steam Trawling & Fishing Co. Ltd. She had been taken up for Naval service as a boom defence vessel only the previous month, and was accidentally sunk by a Naval vessel in Scapa Flow.

21 July 1915   *Briton*   A 101   196 Tons/1906

The *Briton* was built by Hall Russell's for the Standard Steam Fishing Co. Ltd. of Aberdeen. She had been taken up for minesweeping in February 1915 and was mined and sank off the Longsands in the Harwich area. There were only three survivors.

22 July 1915   *Star of Peace*   A 323   180 Tons/1900

The *Star of Peace* was built by Halls for the Walker Steam Trawl Fishing Co. Ltd. She was captured by a U-Boat and sunk by gunfire 114 miles N x W of Hoy Head, Orkney.

24 July 1915   *Strathmore*   A 136   163 Tons/1899

Built by Hall Russell's and owned by the Aberdeen Steam Trawling & Fishing Co. Ltd, the *Strathmore* was captured by a U-Boat and sunk by gunfire 60 miles N x W of Butt of Lewis.

24 July 1915   *Roslin* (1)   A 8   128 Tons/1899

The *Roslin* was built at Montrose for John Lewis, who sold her in 1909 to W. Masson and others. In company with the *Strathmore* she was captured by a U-Boat and sunk by gunfire 60 miles N x W of Butt of Lewis.

6 August 1915   *Ocean Queen*   A 175   185 Tons/1900

Built by Mackie & Thomson of Govan for the Aberdeen Fish Supply Association Ltd, the *Ocean Queen* was captured by a U-Boat and sunk by a bomb placed on board 23 miles N x W of Muckle Flugga, Shetland.

8 August 1915   *Ben Ardna* (1)   A 517   197 Tons/1912

The *Ben Ardna* was owned by Richard Irvin & Sons Ltd. and was taken up for minesweeping at the outbreak of war in August 1914. She was mined and sunk off the Elbow Buoy while in service as a minesweeper.

31 October 1915   *John G. Watson*   A 327   196 Tons/1910

Owned by Richard Irvin & Sons Ltd, the *John G. Watson* was taken up for minesweeping in November 1914. She sank after a collision near Stornoway. A replacement *John G. Watson* was built in 1916, registered SN 305, and immediately taken over by the Navy.

28 November 1915   *William Morrison*   A 355   211 Tons/1915

The *William Morrison* was owned by the Pioneer Steam Fishing Co. Ltd. and named after one of their skippers. Other ships of the company similarly named after skippers were *P. Fannon* (A 349) and *Robert Smith* (A 353) (q.v.). She was mined and sunk near Sunk Head Buoy, off Harwich, while on Naval service as a minesweeper. The ship was only two months old.

2 December 1915   *Jackdaw*   A ?   150 Tons/1895

The *Jackdaw* was on her way to the fishing grounds off Shetland when she was overtaken by a severe storm.

Skipper Thomas Christie made for shelter in Mid Yell Voe on the east side of the island of Yell, but on the way there the *Jackdaw* ran ashore on the south-east side of Burraness Point in Yell. The crew were unable to launch their smallboat and took to the rigging to escape the pounding waves, lashing themselves to the mast to prevent themselves falling into the sea. Several hours later, as daylight came in, a local crofter spotted the wreck and immediately arranged with some of his neighbours to launch his boat and make for the scene. On boarding the *Jackdaw*, the Shetlanders found that the crew were completely helpless after their ordeal and had to be cut free from the rigging. All the crew were safely got ashore, but one, an Englishman named Grey of 235 Victoria Road, died shortly afterwards of exposure. He left a widow and a young family.

6 December 1915   *Philorth*   A 376   139 Tons/1892

The *Philorth* was yet another ex-Fraserburgh trawler owned originally by the Fraserburgh Steam Trawling Co. Ltd. and bought from Dundee owners only in July 1915 by W.H. Dodds, the Aberdeen trawlowner.

A storm of great violence had been raging off the Buchan coast for several days when the *Philorth* was driven ashore by tremendous waves near the Old Castle of Slains, Cruden Bay. There was a strong easterly gale, accompanied by heavy rain showers, when at 6 a.m, farm workers on farms nearby heard the sound of a ship's siren, and in making their way to the shore discovered that the trawler had grounded on a rock known as the Riddle Skerries. She was not burning flares, but it was evident that she was in a serious plight. The darkness was intense, the rain was descending in torrents, and the men on shore could just discern the vessel only a few yards from the shore. Huge waves were breaking over her and it could be seen that she would soon break up. Her stern was stuck fast and every wave lifted her bow high into the air. The crew were huddled round the galley but no assistance could be given until the arrival of the rocket apparatus from Collieston at almost 9 a.m. By this time the trawler was lying on her side and the crew members had taken to the side of the galley. Several lines were fired to the men but to have left the galley would have meant instant death, as no man could have held on in such conditions. At last a line thrown from the shore fell near the galley, and one of the crew, deckhand William Scarborough of Wales Street, Aberdeen, grasping the rudder chain-pipe in his hand secured a firm hold of the line. Taking the line between his teeth, he pulled in about another foot of the rope, and again seized it with his teeth. In this way he drew in the line foot by foot until there was sufficient for his companions to hold on to, and a heavier rope could be brought across to rig the breeches buoy.

By now it was broad daylight, and only six men could be seen on the ship. The first of the crew to get into the breeches buoy was William Scarborough. On his way to the shore he was overwhelmed by a huge wave, the buoy came up empty and Scarborough was not seen again. The first survivor to come ashore was a lad of eighteen, Albert Davidson, son of the second engineer. He was a passenger on the trawler and making his first trip to sea. He was completely exhausted and benumbed with cold and his father had tied a rope round his waist in the breeches buoy before signalling to the rescuers to pull him ashore. He was carried to the farm of Clochtow nearby, but all efforts to revive him failed. He was followed ashore by the chief and second engineers and the cook, and then by the mate, who was in a state of collapse and required medical attention.

The skipper and three other crew members were washed away to their deaths.

Those lost were:-
Skipper James Swanson (30) 33 Victoria Road, a native of Thurso (a widow and one child).
Second fisherman William Ferris, Aberdeen.
Deckhand William Booth, Victoria Road (widow and three children).
Deckhand William Scarborough, Wales Street (single).
Fireman Thomas Collie (50) 45 Guestrow.
Albert Davidson, (18) 36 Victoria Road.

The names of those rescued were:-

Mate William Charman, 64 Gerrard Street (widower).
Ch. Engineer Andrew Thomson, 66 Walker Road.
Second Engineer William Davidson, 36 Victoria Road.
Cook W.W. Jones, 94 Summer Street.

23 December 1915 *Empress* A 289 104 Tons/1890

The *Empress* was a small trawler of only 104 tons, half the size of the average trawler of the time, built in South Shields in 1890 for an Aberdeen owner, Robert Laing, Junior, 82 Union Grove. Mr. Laing sold the vessel to a Hartlepool owner in 1898, and the *Empress* fished from the English port until being brought back to Aberdeen in April 1915, under the ownership of Andrew Walker, of the Walker Steam Trawl Fishing Co. Ltd. All of the modern ships in the Aberdeen fleet had by now been taken up for minesweeping duties in the Royal Navy, so that Aberdeen owners were obliged to seek around in the smaller fishing ports to find ships to take the places of those that were now on Admiralty service.

A severe south-easterly gale was sweeping Scotland's east coast, making fishing impossible and causing any shipping unfortunate enough to be at sea to seek shelter from the mountainous waves or to take what steps they could to ride out the storm at sea. During the forenoon a number of trawlers could be discerned through the driving spray making way cautiously to the entrance of Aberdeen harbour. One by one they ran the gauntlet of the huge seas until they reached the comparative shelter of the harbour channel, when the full extent of the damage they had suffered could be seen by the anxious watchers onshore. Several had had their lifeboats smashed or carried away completely, the large ventilators beside the funnel bent over or missing altogether.

Suddenly, people who were watching the scene from the Balnagask side thought they saw one of the trawlers in difficulties and founder in the waves breaking over the harbour bar, about 300 yards from the South Breakwater, but in the poor visibility they could not be certain that the boat had not merely been thrown off course by a breaking wave and had turned round for another attempt. They had been unable to identify the trawler, and the large amount of flotsam that was accumulating along the Torry shore, in the shape of lifebelts bearing the names of several vessels and even part of a ship's lifeboat, added to the confusion.

The storm continued into the Friday, Christmas Eve, when a Grimsby trawler, the *Cameo*, ran ashore at Rattray Head and was lost with all hands. A small puffer, the *Moor*, belonging to Glasgow, had come through the Forth and Clyde Canal with a cargo of machinery for Dundee, and was making her way into the entrance to the Tay when she was overwhelmed by the huge seas and the opposing tide, and was lost with her crew of four.

At Johnshaven, a Norwegian schooner, the *Ski Bladner*, loaded with pit props and having lost one of her masts, was driven ashore and within a short time was pounded to pieces. One member of the crew was drowned in an attempt to swim ashore, but the remaining six were saved in the nick of time by the Johnshaven life-saving rocket apparatus.

The missing trawler at Aberdeen had still not been identified, and it was suspected from wreckage washed ashore that she was the *Britannia*, six of whose crew were from the Stonehaven area. The storm began to abate late on the Saturday but it was to be Sunday forenoon before trawlers were again able to enter the harbour, and over twenty fishing vessels including the *Britannia*, succeeded in reaching safety. Most of them showed signs of the severe buffeting they had encountered, and many of the crews had had no food for several days.

By the following Wednesday, six days after the tragedy, the only trawler which had been expected home over the weekend and which had not been accounted for was the *Empress*, a small ship built in 1890 and carrying eight of a crew. By this time, too, some of the wreckage on the Torry shore had been identified as belonging to the *Empress*. The ship's medicine chest bearing her name and which was always kept below deck was cast ashore at Balnagask along with the wheelhouse clock and two broken lifebelts, while two masts from a trawler were washed ashore in Greyhope Bay near Girdleness Lighthouse.

The crew were all married men with homes in Aberdeen, though it is interesting that the newspapers stated that "all but the cook are English". It must be remembered, however, that a large number of English fishermen moved to Aberdeen with their families when the trawling boom was at its height some twenty years earlier. It was almost a week before the first body to be identified came ashore, that of a fisherman, a former skipper whose own trawler had been taken over by the Admiralty as a minesweeper and who had shipped as a deckhand on the *Empress*. The skipper, John Barber, who lived in Torry had taken over the *Empress* only three weeks before on account of the illness of her regular skipper, Skipper Wilkinson, one of whose sons, a man of twenty-two, was sailing as second fisherman on the trawler. No less than twenty-six children were left fatherless by the tragedy, made all the more poignant by its having occurred within a quarter of a mile of safety, only two days before Christmas.

2 January 1916 *Mediator* A 483 178 Tons/1912

The *Mediator*, built by Alexander Hall & Co. Ltd. for A. Forbes, 268 Victoria Road, had been taken up for Naval service in September 1914. She was mined off Hornsea, Yorkshire while on Naval service.

15 January 1916 *Braconmoor* (1) A 164 204 Tons/1900

The *Braconmoor* had been sold to North Shields owners and there were no Aberdeen men in the crew. She foundered in the North Sea due to stress of weather and the crew were all landed safely at Grimsby by the trawler *Diamond* (GY 603).

24 January 1916 *Clover Bank* (1) A 379 78 Tons/1912

Built at Sandhaven and owned by Geddes & Co. Ltd. of Aberdeen, the *Clover Bank* was taken up for Naval service in January 1915. She was mined off Zeebrugge while on Naval service. *Clover Bank* was one of a number of drifters owned by Geddes & Company and registered in Aberdeen. Several were built at their own yard in Portgordon, and others at the Forbes Yard in Sandhaven near Fraserburgh. A second *Clover Bank*, to replace the first, was built at Banff in 1917 and immediately taken over by the Royal Navy. Her naval career was tragically short, however, as she was shelled and sunk by German destroyers on 15th February 1918 in the Dover Straits with only one survivor.

12 August 1916 *Welsh Prince* A 280 122 Tons/1895

The *Welsh Prince*, purchased by Andrew Walker from North Shields owners in March 1915, ran ashore in fog at Girdleness Lighthouse while returning from a fishing trip. Her crew of nine succeeded in getting ashore in their smallboat.

4 September 1916 *Jessie Nutten* A 243 187 Tons/1908

The *Jessie Nutten* had been built by Hall Russells for the Nutten family and had been taken up for minesweeping. She was mined and sunk off Lowestoft while on Naval service.

25 September 1916 *Ant* A 308 158 Tons/1891

The *Ant* had been bought in 1910 by J. & R. Moon, Butchers, Torry. She was sunk in collision with S.T. *Osprey* (A 366) two miles off the Cruden Scaurs. The second engineer, James Hedger, was lost and the remaining crew picked up by the *Osprey* which made for Aberdeen. The *Osprey's* engines failed off the Donmouth and she had to be towed stern first to Aberdeen by a naval patrol vessel.

26 September 1916 *Loch Shiel* A 273 216 Tons/1909

The *Loch Shiel* was built by Hall Russells and owned by the Empire Steam Fishing Co. of Aberdeen Ltd. She had been taken up for minesweeping in April 1915 and was mined and sunk off Milford Haven while on Naval service.

22 October 1916 *Effort* A 487 159 Tons/1895

Govan-built and bought from Hull owners in 1912 by Aberdeen owner Thomas Lauder, the *Effort* was captured by a U-Boat and sunk by gunfire thirty miles ENE of Buchan Ness.

8 November 1916 *Vineyard* A 787 126 Tons/1896

Built by Hall Russells in 1896 for the Tullos Steam Fishing Co. Ltd, the *Vineyard* had had several changes of owners, but had continued to fish from Aberdeen. She was mined 13 miles S x E of Buchan Ness with the loss of all eight of her crew.

16 December 1916 *Crathie* (2) A 713 225 Tons/1916

Built to replace the earlier *Crathie*, lost in the first months of the war, the second *Crathie* was immediately taken up for naval service, and was wrecked on Nizam Point, Barra Head, after only one month of service.

7 January 1917 *Donside* A 155 182 Tons/1900

The *Donside* was built by Duthies for George Fyfe, 51 Shiprow and was taken up for minesweeping in August 1914. She was mined and sunk off Lowestoft while on naval service.

21 January 1917 *Deeside* A 397 197 Tons/1900

The *Deeside* was built by Alexander Hall & Co. and was also owned by George Fyfe, owner of the *Donside*. The *Deeside* stranded sixty yards south of Craigewan Point just north of Peterhead. Her crew of ten were saved by the Peterhead Life Saving Apparatus.

21 January 1917 *Star of the Sea* A 538
197 Tons/1902

The *Star of the Sea* was built by Halls for the Walker Steam Trawl Fishing Co. Ltd, who sold her in 1916 to Fleetwood owners. She was captured by a U-Boat and sunk by gunfire forty-three miles NW x N of Inishtrahull Island, north of Ireland.

9 February 1917 *Duke of York* A 422 150 Tons/1893

The *Duke of York*, built in Hull and owned by R.W. Lewis since 1911, was captured by a U-Boat and sunk by bombs placed on board thirty-four miles E x S of Girdleness.

13 February 1917 *Sisters Melville* A 459
260 Tons/1915

The *Sisters Melville* was a new trawler built for Mrs. Ann Melville, 39 Murray Terrace. She was taken up for mine-sweeping immediately on completion and was mined and sunk off Aldeburgh, Suffolk whole on naval service.

4 April 1917 *Maggie Ross* A 449 183 Tons/1901

The *Maggie Ross*, built by Hall Russells, was one of three trawlers built in September 1901 for the Ross steam Trawl Fishing Co. Ltd, the others being the *Jane Ross* (A 454) and the *Harry Ross* (A 453) built by Halls and Hall Russells respectively. The *Maggie Ross* was captured by a U-Boat and sunk by gunfire seventy miles NE of Aberdeen.

6 April 1917 *Strathrannoch* A 752 215 Tons/1917

Completed in January 1917 for the Aberdeen Steam Trawling & Fishing Co. Ltd, the *Strathrannoch* was immediately taken up for minesweeping and was mined and sunk off St. Abbs Head while on naval service.

9 April 1917 *Orthos* A 591 218 Tons/1913

The *Orthos* had been built by Duthies for the National Steam Fishing Co. (Aberdeen) Ltd. She was taken up for minesweeping in August 1914 and was mined and sunk off Lowestoft while on naval service.

12 April 1917 *Chinkiang* A 798 125 Tons/1896

The *Chinkiang* was a small trawler built by Halls for owner James Thom. She had several changes of owner during her career, all of it in Aberdeen. She was captured by a U-Boat and sunk by gunfire thirty miles NE of Buchan Ness.

12 April 1917   *Largo Bay*   A 372   125 Tons/1897

The *Largo Bay* had been built in Dundee for the Bay Fishing Co. Ltd. and registered KY 575. She came to Aberdeen in 1901 and at the time of her loss was owned by the North Star Steam Fishing Co. Ltd. She was captured by a U-Boat and sunk by gunfire thirty miles NE x E of Buchan Ness.

12 April 1917   *Fife Ness*   A 377   123 Tons/1897

Another ex-Kirkcaldy Trawler brought to Aberdeen in 1901, the *Fife Ness* had been built by Hall Russells for the Ness Fishing Co. Ltd. She was owned in Aberdeen by Thomas Davidson and was captured by a U-Boat and sunk by gunfire twenty-three miles ENE of Fraserburgh.

12 April 1917   *Osprey*   A 366   106 Tons/1883

A small trawler built at South Shields, the *Osprey* was previously registered in Scarborough (SH 79) before being bought by Aberdeen owner Andrew Walker in June 1915. She was captured by a U-Boat and sunk by gunfire forty-five miles NE x E of Girdleness.

12 April 1917   *Crown Prince*   A 369   103 Tons/1890

Like the *Osprey*, above, the *Crown Prince* was built in South Shields and was owned by Andrew Walker, who had bought her from Fraserburgh owners in 1915. She was captured by a U-Boat and sunk by gunfire forty-five miles NE x E of Girdleness in the company of the *Osprey* and the *Lillian*.

12 April 1917   *Lillian*   A 603   120 Tons/1894

Built of iron at Beverley, the *Lillian* was previously owned in Buckie before being bought by Andrew Lewis in 1915. In company with the *Osprey* and the *Crown Prince* she was captured by a U-Boat and sunk by gunfire forty-five miles NE x E of Girdleness.

13 April 1917   *Pitstruan*   A 585   206 Tons/1913

Built by Halls for J.S. Doeg, the *Pitstruan* was one of the first Aberdeen trawlers to be taken up for minesweeping on the outbreak of war. She was mined and sunk off Noss Head, Caithness, while on naval service.

20 April 1917   *Loch Eye*   A 693   225 Tons/1916

Completed in July 1916 for the Empire Steam Fishing Co. of Aberdeen Ltd, the *Loch Eye* was immediately taken up for minesweeping and was mined and sunk off Dunmore, County Waterford, while on naval service.

22 April 1917   *Nightingale*   A 556   91 Tons/1892

Another small trawler owned by Andrew Walker, the *Nightingale* had previously been registered in Glasgow (GW 22) before being bought in December 1915. The *Nightingale* was captured by a U-Boat and sunk by a bomb placed on board twenty-six miles south of Aberdeen.

26 April 1917   *Active* (1)   A 776   149 Tons/1892

The *Active*, built and registered in Hull (H 191), was bought from Cornwall owners by H.E. Stroud only in March 1917. She was to have been transferred to Grimsby owners but was sunk before the transaction could be completed. She was captured by a U-Boat and sunk by a bomb placed on board eighty miles ESE of St. Abbs Head.

30 April 1917   *Argo*   A 196   131 Tons/1896

The *Argo* had been built in Hull and was bought from Grimsby owners in 1908. At the time of her loss she was owned by W. Meff & J. Ellis. She was captured by a U-Boat and sunk by gunfire fifteen miles E of Buchan Ness.

(Note: There were two trawlers named *Argo* fishing from Aberdeen from 1913 to 1916. The other *Argo* (A 554) was sold to Grimsby in 1916.)

1 June 1917   *Teal*   A 428   141 Tons/1893

Built at Govan, the *Teal* was previously registered in London (LO 135) before being bought by the Standard

Fishing Co. Ltd. in 1915. She was captured by a U-Boat and sunk by gunfire fifty-seven miles NW x N of Sule Skerry.

26 June 1917   *Taurus*   A 655   128 Tons/1883

The *Taurus*, built at Hull in 1883, was one of the oldest steam trawlers in existence when she was purchased from Grimsby owners by George Craig and others in 1916. Her registration was cancelled on 30th August 1917, as it was believed she was sunk by a mine on 26th June. No further details are available.

10 July 1917   *Vale of Leven*   A 177   223 Tons/1907

The *Vale of Leven* was built by Hall Russells and owned by the Vale of Leven Steam Fishing Co. Ltd. She was taken up for minesweeping in March 1915 and was sunk in collision off Worthing while on naval service.

12 July 1917   *George Milburn*   A 634   235 Tons/1916

Completed by Hall Russells in April 1916 for Richard Irvin & Sons Ltd. the *George Milburn* was immediately taken over by the Admiralty as a minesweeper and was mined and sunk off Dunmore, County Waterford, while on naval service. The *Loch Eye* (A 693), completed three months later was lost in the same minefield.

20 July 1917   *Robert Smith*   A 353   211 Tons/1915

Owned by the Aberdeen Pioneer Steam Fishing Co. Ltd. and named after one of their skippers, the *Robert Smith* was taken up for patrol duties on completion in July 1915 and was armed with both six-pounder and twelve-pounder guns. She disappeared north-west of the Hebrides while on naval service.

10 September 1917   *Loch Ard* (1)   A 503
225 Tons/1912

The *Loch Ard* was owned by the Bon-Accord Steam Fishing Co. Ltd. and had been taken up for minesweeping in August 1914. She was mined and sunk off Lowestoft while on naval service.

8 October 1917   *Ben Heilem*   A 470   196 Tons/1912

The *Ben Heilem*, built by Hall Russells for Richard Irvin & Sons Ltd, was one of the first Aberdeen trawlers to become a minesweeper.

She was armed with both six-pounder and twelve-pounder guns, and was wrecked off Berwick while on naval service.

13 October 1917   *Aster*   A 762   198 Tons/1883

The *Aster*, an old Greenock-built trawler, was bought by George Craig of Aberdeen only in March 1917. She did not return from a fishing trip to Shetland and is believed to have been sunk by mine explosion off Out Skerries, Shetland.

19 November 1917   *Morococala*   A 238
265 Tons/1915

Built for Skipper J.F. Duthie of Buckie, the *Morococala* was taken over for minesweeping immediately on completion in April 1915. She was mined off the Daunt Lightvessel, Southern Ireland, while on naval service.

10 December 1917   *Amadavat*   A 619   171 Tons/1899

The *Amadavat* was bought from Plymouth in 1916 by R. Milne of Aberdeen. She went missing, presumed mined, off Shetland, with the loss of her crew of nine.

21 December 1917   *Ocean Scout* 1   A 362
200 Tons/1915

Built for the Aberdeen Fish Supply Association Ltd, the *Ocean Scout* 1 was immediately taken over for minesweeping. She was sunk in collision off Western Ireland while on naval service.

16 January 1918   *John E Lewis*   A 354   253 Tons/1911

The *John E Lewis*, owned by John Lewis was built by Hall Russells in 1911 to replace an earlier *John E Lewis* (A 294), built by Hall Russells in 1909 and sold to

Portugal in 1910. The second *John E Lewis* was taken up for minesweeping in August 1914 and was mined off the Cork Lightvessel, Harwich while on naval service.

29 January 1918   *Drumtochty*   A 408   211 Tons/1915

The *Drumtochty* was built for the North of Scotland Steam Fishing Co. Ltd. and was taken up by the Navy immediately on completion. She was mined off Dover while on naval service.

**15 February 1918   *Clover Bank* (2)   A 731
92 Tons/1917**

The *Clover Bank* was built to replace the drifter *Clover Bank* (A 379), mined off Zeebrugge on 24th April 1916. She was sunk by German destroyers (along with six other drifters) in the Dover Straits in a night action. There was only one survivor.

28 February 1918   *North West*   A 478   123 Tons/1890

The *North West* was one of no less than six trawlers built in 1890 in Aberdeen for the North Line Fleet of William Pyper, Hillhead, Pitfodels. She was sold to J.A. Harrow in 1907 and had two further changes of owner before her loss. She is entered in the fishing vessels register as "total loss" but no further details have been traced.

10 March 1918   *Endeavour*   A 493   156 Tons/1894

Built at Govan, the *Endeavour* was previously a Hull trawler (H 243) which had been bought by George Craig, Fishcurer, in 1912. Surprisingly, in view of her age, she was taken over by the Admiralty in June 1915 to be a boom defence vessel. She was sunk in collision off Kirkwall while on naval service.

23 March 1918   *New Dawn*   A 221   93 Tons/1908

A steel drifter, built at Govan and owned by the Steam Herring Fleet Ltd. of Aberdeen, the *New Dawn* was commandeered for minesweeping in November 1914.

She was mined and sunk at the entrance to the Needles Channel.

23 April 1918   *Tyne Wave*   A 736   121 Tons/1891

The *Tyne Wave* was a small trawler built at Newcastle and previously registered in North Shields (SN 122). She had been brought to Aberdeen in 1916 by owner Nicholas Cook but was sold to Scarborough owners in March 1918. She was captured by a U-Boat and sunk by gunfire twenty miles WNW of Ramna Stacks, Northmavine, Shetland.

23 April 1918   *Peregrine*   A 895   79 Tons/1877

The *Peregrine* was registered as a fishing vessel only four months earlier by W.J. Duncan and W.A. Leith. She was captured by a U-Boat and sunk by gunfire fifteen miles NNW of Ramna Stacks, Northmavine, Shetland.

23 April 1918   *Plethos*   A 545   210 Tons/1913

The *Plethos*, built by Halls for the East Coast Steam Fishing Co. (Aberdeen) Ltd, had been taken up for minesweeping in September 1914 and was mined off Montrose while on naval service.

13 May 1918   *Loch Naver*   A 45   216 Tons/1906

The *Loch Naver* was built by Halls for the Bon-Accord Steam Fishing Co. Ltd. She was taken over by the Navy in February 1915 and was mined in the Aegean Sea while on naval service.

14 July 1918   *Loch Tummel*   A 494   228 Tons/1912

The *Loch Tummel*, built by Duthies for the Empire Steam Fishing Co. of Aberdeen Ltd. was taken up for minesweeping in April 1915. She foundered in the Mediterranean while on naval service.

19 February 1919   *Sapphire*   A 889   156 Tons/1903

The *Sapphire* had been built by Hall Russells for John Craig of Torry. She served as a minesweeper from August

1914 to November 1918, when she was returned and sold to Scarborough owners. She was sunk by a mine explosion in the North Sea. Her crew were rescued and landed in Hull.

28 September 1919   *Eagle*   A 874   45 Tons/1879

The *Eagle* was a small vessel which had been bought by George Craig, Aberdeen, in October 1917. She had a crew of six and was used for line fishing. She stranded in a gale on the island of Fladday, east of Skye. The crew managed to launch their smallboat and land on the island. A newspaper report at the time stated "As Fladday is uninhabited and the crew had no food or effects, they were compelled to slaughter a sheep they found on the island." It did not disclose how the crew, without "effects" were able to cook or partake of their "meal".

? November 1919   *Cruiser*   A 882   12 Tons/1887

The *Cruiser* was an even smaller vessel, with only five of a crew, brought to Aberdeen in February 1918. She was sold to the Leith Pilots Association and was a total loss in November 1919. No further details can be traced.

9 March 1920   *Cepheus*   A 656   155 Tons/1891

The *Cepheus* came to Aberdeen with the trawler *Taurus* (A 655) (q.v.) in 1916 under the ownership of George Craig and others. She was on her way to the fishing grounds when she ran aground near the old breakwater in the entrance channel to Aberdeen Harbour. The crew were at first in no danger, and remained on board, expecting that their ship would refloat at high tide. As the tide rose, however, the ship filled with water until only the funnel, masts and wheelhouse were visible. The crew launched their own smallboat and rowed to safety. The trawler *Leven* (A 447), which had run aground at the same spot two days previously, had succeeded in refloating herself that morning, and proceeded under her own steam to the fish market to land her fish.

12 March 1920   *Ray*   A 917   21 Tons/1898

The *Ray* was a small steam vessel which had been brought to Aberdeen in 1918 when anything that floated was pressed into service to augment the nation's food supply. She appears not to have been particularly successful as a fishing vessel as she had been laid up at Aberdeen for some time prior to her loss. She was returning to Aberdeen after an overnight fishing trip when she encountered a severe gale and began to fill with water. Her distress flares were seen by the local trawler *H. E. Stroud* (A270) which immediately went to her assistance. The crew were rescued by the *H E Stroud* and brought to Aberdeen. In the meantime, Newburgh lifeboat had been launched in response to the *Ray's* distress flares and reached the foundering trawler, only to find that the crew had already been rescued.

5 October 1920   *Glengarry*   A 207   64 Tons/1900
Glenshee   A 386   67 Tons/1901

These two steam drifters were stranded on Aberdeen beach when, along with several trawlers, they broke adrift from their moorings at Point Law in a heavy spate on the river Dee and were swept out to sea.

10 October 1920   *Ben Namur*   A 244   224 Tons/1919

The *Ben Namur*, only a year old, ran ashore in a thick fog and heavy swell early on a Sunday morning on the west side of the Orkney mainland, two miles north of the Bay of Skaill. The mate, Alexander Lawrence, 37 Victoria Road, and a deckhand, Alexander Cordiner, 27 Skene Street, were swept overboard and drowned. By sounding the trawler's siren and burning flares, people were attracted to the scene and a line attached to a water cask was floated ashore by the fishermen, eight of whom managed to land safely, although one of them sustained a severe leg injury. The line broke before the last man, the skipper, William Coates, could be rescued.

However, the Stromness Rocket Brigade arrived shortly afterwards and their first rocket put a line over the trawler, enabling the skipper to be brought ashore by breeches buoy. All except the skipper left Stromness for Aberdeen the same evening by the steamer *St Clair* which had been delayed for two days by the severe weather.

30 November 1920   *Breadalbane*   A 281
112 tons/1891

The *Breadalbane* had been built at Bowling on the Clyde for the General Steam Fishing Co. Ltd. of Granton and registered GN 32. She was bought by Thomas Wood & others in 1920. She was wrecked outside Lossiemouth harbour and her crew saved by the local life saving apparatus.

27 November 1921   *Keith Hall*   A 636   152 Tons/1896

The *Keith Hall* was formerly the German trawler *Darmstadt*, which had been captured by HMS *Cleopatra* on 30th September 1915. Taken over by the Navy in October 1915, she was re-named *Carbosin* and served in the Navy until October 1920, when she was sold to Aberdeen owners (Ellis & Meff), who used her as a steam line-fishing vessel.

On her way home after a fishing trip to Faroe, she ran ashore in fog at Birsay, Orkney, at 5.20 pm on a Sunday evening. Locals at Birsay sent a telegram to Stromness requesting the lifeboat and rocket apparatus to proceed to the scene. When the telegram arrived, the men were at a service in the parish church and some time was lost in getting the crew together. Several of the lifeboatmen ran from the church direct to their boat, while the rocket men got vehicles to transport their gear to the scene. The rocket Company were the first to arrive, only to find that the crew had left in their own boat, and were keeping some distance off the land. The lifeboat crew, when they arrived, spotted a light to seaward of the wreck, and this proved to be the boat with the crew on board, all except one man, George Neilson of 114 Walker Road, who had been washed overboard while assisting in the launch of the smallboat. The crew, under Skipper William King, were picked up by the lifeboat and taken to Stromness.

28 December 1921   *Joseph Hodgkins*   A 186
276 Tons/1919

The *Joseph Hodgkins* had been built by Hepple & Co. Ltd, South Shields as an Admiralty Castle-class trawler. She was too late for naval service and was sold to F.R. Samson of London. Although registered in Aberdeen, it is doubtful whether she ever fished from the port. She was sunk in collision with the Grimsby trawler *Cuirasse* (GY 436) off Maughold Head, Isle of Man.

3 February 1922   *Curlew*   A 906   125 Tons/1897

The *Curlew* had been built in Dundee for Dundee owners and took the registration DE 91 until she was brought to Aberdeen by A.W. Ritchie of Torry and registered in Aberdeen in September 1903. She was sold to Skipper Andrew King in 1907 and was indeed under his command when she was lost. She was entering Aberdeen Harbour in a severe south-easterly gale when she ran aground on the south side of the entrance channel. Skipper King of 56 Grampian Road, and his crew of nine, were rescued by Torry Life-saving Brigade and the *Curlew* became a total loss. She was replaced the following month by Skipper King, who bought the Aberdeen-built Granton trawler *Granton NB* (GN 78). She took the registration of the old *Curlew* and was renamed *Curlew* in April 1922.

8 October 1922   *Lady Betty Balfour*   A 864
53 Tons/1898

The *Lady Betty Balfour* was one of the last survivors of the small trawlers which Aberdeen owners had bought in the last two years of the war. She was owned by Captain Nicholas Cook who had just bought the ill-fated trawler *George* when she was lost on 3rd January 1911. The *Lady Betty Balfour* had been based on Mallaig for some six months and was returning there with her catch when she began to founder. The crew of six took to their smallboat and had barely got clear when the trawler's carbide tank exploded, setting fire to the ship, which was

Keith Hall – The **Keith Hall** (A 636) on the rocks near Birsay, Orkney, after running ashore in fog on 27 November 1921. Her long black funnel shows her to be a former German trawler. She had been captured by the Royal Navy in 1915 and had spent the rest of World War I as a minesweeper. At the time of her loss she was employed as a line fishing vessel. (Photo George Coull Collection).

Drumblade – The **Drumblade** when new in 1900. She is fitted for line fishing, without winch or gallows. She was H.M.S. **Drumblade** from 1914 to 1919, and was wrecked at Papa Westray, Orkney on 22 May 1924. (Photo Aberdeen Museum).

burning furiously when she sank. The crew were able to row to Canna Island, from where they were taken to Mallaig by boat.

19 October 1923 *Imperial Prince* A 146
128 Tons/1899

The *Imperial Prince* was one of Aberdeen's smaller trawlers, brought to Aberdeen from North Shields in 1914 along with her sisters *African Prince* and *Fisher Prince*. She worked the nearer fishing grounds of the North Sea, never more than a few hours steaming from Aberdeen, and normally would have landed her fish once or twice a week. She had left the fishing grounds at midnight, and at 6 am, in thick weather with a heavy swell runnning, she grounded on a sandbank some 400 yards off the coast at Black Dog about five miles north of Aberdeen. Her distress flares were spotted by a local farmer, Adam Buchan, Easter Hatton, Millden, who informed the police at Balmedie, and they in turn passed the message to the nearby Belhelvie and Bridge of Don Coastguards. It was 8.30 am before the lifesaving apparatus could reach the shore nearest to the trawler. The crew of nine had taken to the rigging, and only the masts and funnel were visible. After several attempts, the coastguards finally succeeded in placing a rocket line over the *Imperial Prince*, but the survivors were unable to cross the submerged deck to retrieve it.

About 11 am the Aberdeen pulling and sailing lifeboat *Bon Accord 11*, towed by the paddle tug *Monarch*, reached the scene and immediately attempted to get alongside the wreck. The lifeboat had no drogue to keep her head to sea, and as a result broached to before she could reach the *Imperial Prince*. Four of her crew were carried overboard, along with all the oars, but fortunately the remainder of the crew succeeded in rescuing their colleagues and bringing them on board again. Without oars or other method of propulsion, the lifeboat was completely at the mercy of the angry seas and was driven ashore one and a half miles north of the wreck.

At this stage, about midday, the coastguards resumed firing rockets, and one finally fell close to the foremast. One of the deckhands climbed down the rigging to secure the line, lost his footing and fell into the sea. He disappeared from sight and was drowned. Another rocket fell even closer, and this one the trawlermen succeeded in making fast to the mast. As their eyes were sore from the continuous drenching with seawater they had undergone they were unable to read the instructions signalled to them from shore and they were too exhausted to haul out the heavier gear which would have provided the means of getting them to safety.

The Newburgh pulling and sailing lifeboat next arrived on the scene at about 1 pm after being pulled on its cradle for 5 miles along the beach by a farmer's horses and local villagers. The Newburgh men launched their boat some distance south of the wreck to allow for wind and tide but were repeatedly beaten back from the trawler by the heavy seas, until, in a state of near-exhaustion, they finally succeeded in making fast to the wreck by means of a grapnel. They were able to attach a breeches buoy to the rocket line still hanging from the mast, and this was pulled in by the trawler's mate William Shaw, 14 Grampian Road. Three men then made to make the hazardous journey across to the lifeboat. The first man succeeded in getting into the boat, but the second, a deckhand, Duncan Smith, aged 23, fell from the breeches buoy and was lost. As the third man, the Chief Engineer Carl Simon, was got across the line was carried away and the lifeboat came ashore with the two survivors leaving five men still clinging to the rigging. Coxswain Innes of the Newburgh boat got together a crew of lifeboatmen and volunteers and took the boat out again, but was unable to get near the wreck.

About 4 pm, when it was evident that the services on the spot were in an exhausted state, the Peterhead motor lifeboat was called for. Before she arrived, however, a reinforcement of Aberdeen lifeboatmen arrived by bus and the Aberdeen lifeboat was pulled out again, but the fresh oarsmen were unable to make any headway against the battering waves. Just before 6 pm, as darkness was coming down, a party of sailors from HMS *Vampire* and HMS *Vendetta*, destroyers which happened to be visiting Aberdeen, arrived by taxi and it was decided to take the Newburgh lifeboat out again, with three Newburgh men as pilots and the sailors as oarsmen. They pulled straight out to sea and succeeded in getting alongside the wreck by means of a grapnel. The five remaining trawlermen were safely taken off and brought back to shore, only fifteen minutes after the lifeboat had left the beach.

1 April 1924 *Kingfisher* A 613 76 Tons/1882

The *Kingfisher* was a wooden vessel built by Hawthorns of Granton for Granton owners and registered GN 4. She was bought by Alex Robb, Torry, in 1916 and after several changes of ownership her registration was cancelled with the comment "Foundered in Oban bay". No further details have been found.

22 May 1924 *Drumblade* A 133 195 Tons/1900

The *Drumblade* had been built at Montrose for the North of Scotland Steam Fishing Co. Ltd. and had been in the Navy throughout the war, first as a minesweeper and later as a boom defence vessel. She was wrecked at Mull Head, Papa Westray, Orkney. The crew were reported safe.

31 July 1924 *Craigendarroch* A 51 198 Tons/1910

The *Craigendarroch* was formerly the North Shields trawler *John C Meikle* (SN 70), built by Hall Russells in 1910 and bought by Aberdeen owners in March, 1914 being renamed *Craigendarroch* in July 1914. Called up by the Navy in 1915, she became a boom defence vessel for the remainder of the war, being returned to her owners in 1919. In the following year she was sold back to North Shields, but retained her Aberdeen registration.

Between one and two o'clock in the morning of the 31st July 1924, the *Craigendarroch* was on her way to Aberdeen to get a man to complete her crew before proceeding to the West coast fishing grounds. It had been foggy for the whole of the previous day and she was steaming at reduced speed in the thick weather when she grounded in the Outer Neuk, a ledge of rocks just off Portlethen six miles south of Aberdeen. The fisher folks of Portlethen were wakened by the insistent blasts of her siren, and soon the whole of the little village was astir. Through the gloom could be seen the glow of burning flares on the trawler. Launching his boat from the beach about 200 yards from the *Craigendarroch*, a local fisherman, George Craig, with his son, George, and a neighbour Alexander Craig, rowed out and got alongside the trawler just as the crew were launching their own smallboat to come ashore. They took four of the trawler's crew of nine to the beach, and on their return for the others, came upon another crew who were in an even worse plight. This was the crew of the Banff drifter *Lustre Gem* (BF 526), a wooden vessel built by Stephens of Banff in 1907, which had been on a white-fishing trip using a seine net and was making for Aberdeen in the fog with a good catch of flat fish when she struck a rock just after 2 am. The drifter floated off shortly afterwards, but she was making water rapidly and was obviously sinking. Through the fog to the northward could be seen a light, and it was decided to make for it to get assistance. The light turned out to be from the *Craigendarroch*, and as they approached her, the *Craigendarroch* crew shouted "Go astern. We are ashore." The drifter backed off, but by now she was sinking fast and, ultimately, in less than half an hour from the time of striking the rock, she sank off the Downies, only the tops of her masts being visible at low water. The drifter's crew had launched their smallboat and now took to it but their troubles were far from over as water was pouring into the boat through the plughole, and one man used his handkerchief to try to stem the flow. By the time they reached the beach, guided by the Craigs, the boat was three-quarters full of water, but all the crew managed to land safely.

The safe rescue of the crews of the *Craigendarroch* and *Lustre Gem* contrasts sharply with a tragedy which occurred in almost the same place less than four months later. On 28th November 1924, the little wooden drifter *Press Home* (BCK 7), belonging to the fishing village of Portgordon and built there in 1908, was on her way home in thick weather from a successful East Anglian fishing trip, when she ran on to rocks near the Mouches Rock, off Portlethen. Realising that the drifter would soon break up, Skipper Alex Coull of 41 Gordon Street, Portgordon, sounded the siren to attract attention from the shore and shouted to his crew to clamber on to the nearest rocks. The skipper, mate and a deckhand succeeded in getting on to a rock, but the five other members of the crew, including the cook, a boy of sixteen, were swept away and drowned. Meanwhile, a farm servant at the farm of Mains of Portlethen, had heard the siren and raised the alarm, and telephone messages were sent to the Muchalls coastguard and to both the Aberdeen and Stonehaven lifeboats.

George Craig, a seventy year old Portlethen fisherman, had been roused by his son, who lived close by, and immediately made his way down the cliffs to the beach. Another George Craig, of 60 Portlethen, brought a rope and they tried to throw this to the three fishermen, but an intervening boulder frustrated their attempts. Undaunted, "old" George Craig, who knew the rocks intimately, volunteered to clamber out to the intervening rock and to try to reach the men from there. The rock was some twenty-five feet away, but he knew submerged boulders by which he could make his way. The water was waist deep, and sometimes reaching to his neck, but he made his way over to the rock with the rope and succeeded in throwing it to the survivors, one of whom was in poor shape from exposure and the others shouted to get him over first. They tied the rope round his waist and Craig pulled him over to the rock on which he stood, repeating his efforts twice more till all four were on his rock. He shouted to the watchers on shore, and one by one all four were pulled to safety. Craig was presented with the Silver Medal for Gallantry at Sea by King George V at Buckingham Palace, and was also awarded the RNLI Silver Medal.

4 September 1924 *Scottish Belle* A 512 145 Tons/1890

The *Scottish Belle* had been built by J. Scott & Co. Kinghorn for owner Robert Brown. She had been taken over in June 1915 to be a boom defence vessel till 1919. She stranded in fog on the Roan Rocks, Peterhead. Her crew got safely ashore.

5 October 1924 *Strathbran* (2) A 536 212 Tons/1915

The *Strathbran* was one of four trawlers built by Hall Russells in 1915 for John Brown's Aberdeen Steam Trawling & Fishing Co. Ltd, the others being the *Strathelliot* (A 46), the *Strathgairn* (A 251) and the *Strathdevon* (A 539). The *Strathbran* stranded in fog half a mile south of Scotstoun Head. Her crew got safely ashore.

23 January 1925 *Ulster* A 337 185 Tons/1897

The *Ulster*, a steam liner, sailed from Aberdeen between 11 pm and midnight on her way to Granton for coal, after which she was to proceed direct to the fishing grounds. Less than two hours later, she ran aground on to rocks at the foot of the cliffs at Earnsheugh Bay, between Cove and Portlethen, some five miles south of Aberdeen. The skipper, Alexander Robertson of 9 Abbey Place, Torry, ordered the siren to be sounded to attract attention ashore, but after only two blasts the inrushing water put out the boiler fires, cutting off the steam supply. In the thick mist which prevailed, the trawler's position could not be ascertained, so the skipper called the crew to go aft, presumably to launch the smallboat. Three members of the crew, however, led by the second fisherman, Charles Ross of 8 Walker Place, Torry, decided to try to get on to the rocks which could be seen near the trawler's bow. By means of a rope they succeeded in getting ashore and began to scramble over the rocks in an effort to reach safety. The oldest of the three, a deckhand Charles Robertson, 140 Walker Road, whose son of the same name was mate on the vessel, felt unable to continue, so his crewmates left him on a rock out of reach of the sea and continued their struggle to safety, both of them in their bare feet. Arriving at the foot of the precipitous cliffs, they commenced an ascent that, as a newspaper commented, even the most daring would have hesitated at in daylight, for the cliffs were one hundred feet high, sixty feet of which were almost perpendicular. By tremendous efforts, both succeeded in reaching the top and after a breathing space staggered across stubble fields to the farm of Blackhills, Cairnrobin, where they were met by Mrs Knowles, the farmer's wife, who was amazed at their pitiable appearance, being soaking wet, barefoot and with feet, legs and hands cut and bleeding.

A message was at once sent to the Cove coastguard officer, who in turn, called out John Ritchie of the local life-saving crew, and both of them went by motor-cycle and sidecar to the scene of the wreck, carrying their equipment with them. At the clifftop they were joined by the third survivor, deckhand Alexander Craig also of 8 Walker Place, Torry, who had returned to the shore. Craig had, in fact, been the hero of an earlier shipwreck, some thirteen years before, when he scrambled over rocks at Girdleness to rescue the messboy of the Danish ship *G. Koch*, which was being pounded to pieces on the rocks.

The three now scrambled down the cliffs to a ledge from where they were able to throw a line to Robertson, who was still on the boulder where his companions had left him several hours earlier. Robertson tied the rope around his waist and scrambled to the foot of the cliffs to be hauled up slowly, in a state of utter exhaustion, by his three rescuers.

The other five crewmen were all lost. At the public inquiry into the loss of the *Ulster*, it was stated in evidence that the ship was ready to sail at 7 pm, but the mate was missing. When he did turn up at 10.30 pm, he appeared to be under the influence of drink and had a violent row with the cook, as a result of which the cook left, taking his gear with him, and the ship sailed one crewman short. The mate took over the watch at 12.30 am and was the only one in the wheelhouse when the trawler went ashore. When the crew members got to the wheelhouse, the mate was found sound asleep with the engines still going full ahead. The jury's verdict was that the loss had been caused by the negligence of the mate while on duty.

19 December 1925 *Lonicera* A 91 78 Tons/1911

The *Lonicera*, a wooden drifter purchased from Banff owners in May 1925, was stranded off Hartlepool and had her registration cancelled in December 1925. Details of her loss have not been traced.

10 January 1926 *Star of the Wave* A 913 205 Tons/1904

The *Star of the Wave* was returning to Aberdeen with a catch of seventy boxes of fish on a Sunday evening after a three-day trip. A south-easterly gale had sprung up with heavy seas, and a thick haze hung over the land, obscuring all shore lights. William Stewart, the second fisherman and Alex Guyan, a deckhand, were on watch in the wheelhouse, peering anxiously through the haze and the driven spray for a sight of Girdleness light. Stewart was under the impression that the ship had run the required distance and had just roused Skipper John McLeod when the vessel was brought up with a severe jolt, which wakened the sleeping crew. She had driven on to a sandbank off Belhelvie, eleven miles north of Aberdeen. The crew all rushed on deck, aware that the ship had stranded, and every effort was made to extricate her from her position. The engines were put to full astern, but the ship was firmly embedded in the sand and beginning to develop an alarming list. Water was pouring into the ship, and she was settling deep in the surf. A flare was lit, and the siren blown repeatedly. Now it was a case of every man for himself, and half of the crew of ten took to the foremast rigging, and the other five to the wheelhouse.

Huge breakers were sweeping over the trawler, everything moveable on deck, including the smallboat and ventilators, were washed away, and those in the rigging had to cling for their lives. The men in the tiny wheelhouse were in an even more dangerous position. With almost every wave the small space was filled with water, the men being occasionally up to their eyes in the water until it would drain off through the windows and door. The danger to the men was increased by overcrowding, so to relieve the situation, the Chief Engineer, Nicholas Buchanan of 17 Roslin Street, waited for a suitable opportunity to make a dash for the rigging. As soon as he reached the deck, however, he was caught by a huge wave and swept overboard, never to be seen again. A man of forty-seven, he left a widow and a family of five.

The Newburgh pulling lifeboat now arrived, having been pulled along the sands on its four wheeled cradle, and was launched into the surf, but the lifeboatmen were unable to get close enough to the trawler and had to return to the beach after a desperate fight against wind and sea. The Balmedie life-saving crew were also on the scene, and had been firing rockets towards the wreck. At last, some hours after the trawler had grounded and the tide had begun to ebb, a rocket was sent right over the trawler. Shouts told the rescuers that the line had been secured. In about fifteen minutes the apparatus had been fully rigged, and one by one the nine survivors were brought ashore. The *Press & Journal* reported that "the rescue can be put down as one of the cleanest and smartest bits of work of its kind that has taken place along the coast for many a day." The Aberdeen pulling and sailing lifeboat had also been alerted, and left at 12.15 am under Coxswain Tom Sinclair, in tow of the tug *Monarch*. Once clear of the tug, the lifeboatmen began a fierce battle with the wind and heavy seas, only to find that, as she neared the wreck, the water was too shallow to allow an approach, so the lifeboat stood by until she was signalled from the shore to proceed back to Aberdeen. The severe conditions made the return passage much more difficult than the outward one, with the result that it was 7.15 am before her exhausted crew finally reached the safety of Aberdeen harbour.

10 February 1926   *Emperor*   A 610   130 Tons/1895

The *Emperor*, bought second-hand from Dublin by Andrew Walker in 1921, was sunk in collision ten miles off Aberdeen with the Aberdeen trawler *Ocean Prince* (A 576). The crew of nine took to their smallboat and were picked up by the *Ocean Prince*.

28 November 1926   *Caersin*   A 427   128 Tons/1892

The *Caersin* foundered seven miles NE of Aberdeen after a collision in the Moray Firth with the Aberdeen trawler *Cambrisin* (A 426). The *Cambrisin* took the *Caersin* in tow and was within sight of Aberdeen when the *Caersin* sank. The crew were rescued by the *Cambrisin*.

Both ships belonged to the same owner, Nicholas Cook, and both were ex-German trawlers which had been captured by the Royal Navy on the same day in 1915 and employed as minesweepers until the end of the war. The *Caersin* was formerly the German *Dora*, captured by HMS *Penelope*, and the *Cambrisin* was the German *Orion*, captured by HMS *Cleopatra*, both on 30th September 1915.

24 January 1927   *Bravo*   A 305   137 Tons/1896

The *Bravo*, built by Earles of Hull, was previously owned in Lossiemouth (INS 516) and was bought in 1908 by George Wood of Torry. She was used as a steam liner and sank eight miles off Munken, Sydero Island, Faroes. Her crew, all from Torry, under Skipper James H. Walker, were rescued by the local motor boat *Neytul*.

9 May 1927   *Evening Star* (2)   A 406   105 Tons/1891

The *Evening Star* was hauling in her trawl while fishing at the entrance to the Firth of Forth when she sustained damage from the trawl and began to founder. Her crew got away safely in the smallboat and rowed to Dunbar. The trawler had been owned in Leith since 1924, but retained her Aberdeen registration.

She had been built by Eltringhams of South Shields as

the *Ella* for North Shields owners, who sold her to Portknockie in 1907. She came to Aberdeen in 1915, was re-named *Golden Monarch* (A 406) and owned by W.H. Dodds, who sold her to Alex Ritchie of Torry to replace the *Evening Star* (A 530), which had been sunk by a U-Boat in 1915.

6 September 1927   *Ben Torc*   A 604   199 Tons/1913

Shortly before 10 pm, in fog and with a strong south-easterly wind the *Ben Torc*, returning from a coaling trip to Granton with a "scratch" crew of five, went on to the rocks at Gregness, about half a mile south of Girdleness lighthouse. Skipper George Rose sounded the siren continuously and coastguards from the nearby Gregness station were soon on the scene. Two of the coastguards swam across a gully to pass a line to the crew and succeeded in this at the second attempt, although both were badly bruised. However, the crew refused the lifeline and instead called for the lifeboat. The Aberdeen lifeboat *Emma Constance* had recently arrived on station from her builders and she set out at 10.27 pm on what was only her second mission. Coxswain Tom Sinclair used his searchlight to show up the rocks surrounding the wreck and threaded his way in to come alongside the *Ben Torc's* starboard bow.

Five crewmen quickly jumped on to the lifeboat, but Skipper Rose fell into the sea and had to be rescued by line, still wearing his bowler hat!

The *Emma Constance's* first mission had been to the Aberdeen trawler *Venetia* which ran ashore at Girdleness on 21st July 1927 but her services were not required. The *Venetia* was to be lost in tragic circumstances near Stonehaven on 1st/2nd January 1933.

17 November 1927   *Procyon*   A 899   196 Tons/1903

The *Procyon* was built by Hall Russells as the *Strathmartin* for the Aberdeen Steam Trawling & Fishing Co. Ltd. She was sold in 1913 to George Wood who re-named her *Procyon*. She was sunk in collision with the Icelandic steam trawler *Mai* eight miles ENE of Rattray Head. Her crew were taken to Fraserburgh by the *Mai*, and rowed into the harbour in their own smallboat.

6 January 1928   *Strathclunie*   A 583   213 Tons/1913

The *Strathclunie* was returning from a Shetland fishing trip with 180 boxes of fish when she was in collision, eight miles off Buchan Ness, with the Dundee steam trawler *Tumby* (DE 10), which crashed into her starboard side between the fishroom and the bunkers. Water poured into her and so quickly did she start to sink that the crew, under Skipper William Wright, 38 Braemar Place, had no time to launch the smallboat. The skipper of the *Tumby* brought the stern of his vessel close to the fast sinking *Strathclunie*, so that the nine crewmen were able to scramble aboard the *Tumby*. As the last man boarded the *Tumby*, the *Strathclunie* sank head first, taking all the crew's belongings, as well as a good catch of fish, with her, only twenty minutes after the collision.

21 January 1928   *Gladwyn*   A 949   458 Tons/1913

The *Gladwyn* was a large trawler by Aberdeen standards and had been fishing from Hull with a Hull crew. She struck a reef off Sandgerdi, Reykjanes, Iceland in a gale and snowstorm at 10 pm. She fired distress rockets to attract attention and the crew of thirteen were rescued by ropes thrown to them by Icelanders. The trawler broke up two days later.

26 January 1928   *Belmont*   A 101   209 Tons/1906

The *Belmont* had called in at Peterhead harbour during the forenoon and had sailed again about 3 pm. As she crossed the bar into the open sea she was struck by huge waves and, despite all the efforts of the crew, was driven broadside on to the Horseback Rocks, twenty yards from the lifeboat slipway. The propeller was broken off and the trawler badly holed.

Anxious watchers at the harbour had followed the *Belmont's* perilous course through the waves, and as soon as she struck, rockets were fired to call the life-saving brigade crew, who were on the scene within minutes, by which time the *Belmont* was listing dangerously. The first rocket from the brigade successfully straddled the ship and the breeches buoy was rigged to take off the crew of ten. First ashore, however, was the ship's dog, to be followed by five crew members. At this point, the skipper, James Sinkins of 7 Hanover Lane, shouted that he thought that the ship could be towed off and that he and the rest of the crew would remain on board to see whether assistance could be obtained. He changed his mind when the *Belmont* continued to keel over, and followed the others ashore on the breeches buoy. Eventually, the *Belmont* rolled over on to her beam ends and was broken up as she lay.

2 March 1928   *William Butler*   A 695   203 Tons/1917

The *William Butler* had been built for the Admiralty by Hall Russells in 1917, one of almost five hundred trawlers ordered to replace wartime losses and to avoid the need to deplete further the fishing industry, most of whose vessels had by then been requisitioned. All five hundred vessels took their names from the crews of the one-hundred gun ships *Victory* and *Royal Sovereign* at the time of the Battle of Trafalgar. The *William Butler* had retained the name after being sold out of the Navy in 1921.

With her crew of ten, under Skipper John Wood, 39 Menzies Road, she was returning from a seven-day trip to the Scourie Bank, off Scotland's West Coast, with a catch of 160 boxes of haddocks and twenty score of cod, when, in dense fog, she ran on to rocks at the North Head, near the entrance to Peterhead harbour. The Peterhead rocket brigade were quickly on the scene, and had to carry their equipment for some distance over rocks before setting it up on a derelict Admiralty crane barge which had been wrecked some years previously. With spray breaking over them continuously, they were successful in making contact with the trawler with their first rocket. The ten crew were brought ashore safely by breeches buoy.

25 March 1928   *Renaissance*   A 314   199 Tons/1913

Dense fog blanketed the coast from the Moray Firth round to the south of Stonehaven over a weekend during which three trawlers, the *Renaissance* and the *Star of Britain* of Aberdeen, and the *Firsby* of Boston, with a Granton crew, ran ashore in the Peterhead area. In addition to these misfortunes, the Granton trawler *Parkmore*, with four hundred boxes of fish on board, ran ashore near Gardenstown, Banffshire, and was towed off by the drifter *Replenish*, while at Stonehaven the Norwegian cargo steamer *Echo* ran ashore at Strathlethen Bay and became a total loss, fortunately without loss of life.

The *Renaissance* had been built by Hall Russells as the *John H Irvin* (A 593) for Richard Irvin & Sons Ltd, North Shields. After wartime service as a boom defence vessel, she was sold to Scarborough in 1920 and registered SH 190. She had been bought by Andrew Robertson only in January 1928.

She was coming home from an eleven-day trip to the Shetland grounds when she went ashore on rocks at Craigewan Point, two miles north of Peterhead. The Skipper, Robert Allan of 62 Walker Road, Aberdeen, decided to lay a kedge anchor with the intention of pulling the trawler off, and the mate and three members of the crew manned the smallboat to lay the anchor. The anchor was made fast to the smallboat's stern, and the four men were rowing away when a lump of sea capsized the boat, throwing the men into the water. With the weight of the anchor, the boat sank immediately.

The mate, A.J. Smith, of 89 Menzies Road, and two crewmen, both from Buckie, were swept away and disappeared, while the fourth, J.A. Farquhar, the second fisherman, was heard shouting, but his crewmates aboard the *Renaissance* were powerless to reach him. Shortly afterwards, the Peterhead rocket brigade arrived, having forded the River Ugie near its mouth with their apparatus pulled by four horses. This was their third callout to Aberdeen trawlers within two months and they were again successful in getting their first rocket right over the trawler. Just at that moment, the Peterhead lifeboat, under Coxswain John Strachan, arrived alongside the *Renaissance*, and the six remaining members of crew quickly got aboard her. On her way to the wreck, the lifeboatmen heard a faint cry from the fog and were able to discern a man in the water, clinging so desperately to an oar that they had great difficulty in getting him to release his hold. This was the second fisherman, Farquhar, who had drifted half a mile from the wreck and was on the point of exhaustion. The lifeboatmen administered first aid and provided Farquhar with dry clothing. The widows of two of the dead, the mate A.J. Smith and deckhand Peter Cowie, 2 Seatown, Buckie, were sisters, who had five children between them, and the third, the cook, D. Clark of 3 Gordon Street, Buckie, left a widow and four children.

(Later that day the Aberdeen trawler *Star of Britain* grounded off Rattray Head on her way to Aberdeen after a fishing trip to Shetland. Her crew of ten, under Skipper Adam Ferguson, were rescued by breeches buoy by the Rattray rocket brigade. The *Star of Britain* was later salvaged.)

27 March 1928   *Ben Rinnes*   A 488   183 Tons/1901

The third Aberdeen trawler to be lost within the month of March 1928 was the *Ben Rinnes*, built by Hall Russells in 1901 for the North British Steam Fishing Co. Ltd, later Richard Irvin & Sons Ltd. who sold her in 1912 to Thomas Davidson of Aberdeen. During the war she had served as a boom defence vessel and was again sold in 1922, this time to George Craig of Aberdeen. She ran ashore in fog a quarter of a mile west of Spear Point, behind Holborn Head at Scrabster. Her crew were reported safe, but no details of their rescue are available.

17 April 1928   *Strathmoray*   A 480   209 Tons/1912

The *Strathmoray*, under Skipper W.B. Knowles, had set out from Aberdeen on a west-coast fishing trip. Two days fishing at the Flannan Isles brought no luck, so the skipper moved to the Butt of Lewis, where a day's fishing

brought no better result. A gale got up, with frequent snow showers, so Skipper Knowles decided to make for the island of North Rona, about forty miles to the north east. While riding out the gale in the lee of the island, the *Strathmoray* struck a submerged rock a third of a mile from the steep cliffs of North Rona. Other trawlers were sheltering in the vicinity and the Aberdeen trawler *Avonglen* (A 137) (Skipper George Leslie) immediately stood by the stricken *Strathmoray*. The *Strathmoray's* crew launched their smallboat and a towrope was passed from the *Avonglen*, which began to tow the *Strathmoray* towards shallow water. The *Strathmoray* was filling rapidly, however, and her crew had barely time to get into their smallboat when she keeled over and sank into twenty-five fathoms of water. The *Avonglen* picked up the *Strathmoray's* crew and took them to Stromness.

4 October 1928   *Festing Grindall*   A 630
236 Tons/1917

This peculiarly-named trawler, and the trawler *John Gillman*, also later to be Aberdeen registered, were the first of the Castle class of Admiralty trawlers named after the crew of two of Nelson's ships at the Battle of Trafalgar. Both were launched on the same day, 9th January 1917, from the same yard, Smiths Dock Co. Ltd. of Middlesbrough. Both were employed as minesweepers until they were sold by the Admiralty in 1920, when they were bought by Richard W. Lewis, Trawlowner, and both retained their original names. The *Festing Grindall* was on a trip to Granton for coal with a fishing crew of eight under Skipper Joseph Bowie when she ran on to rocks at Fife Ness, in fog. The crew launched their own smallboat and rowed to the nearby Balcomie Sands where they landed safely.

12 May 1929   *Loch Esk*   A 241   215 Tons/1908

The *Loch Esk* was fishing to the west of the Pentland Firth when she was in collision with the German trawler *Hede Sprenger*, which was returning from a trip to Iceland. The *Loch Esk* was severely damaged, but the

Loch Esk – The **Loch Esk** *on her trial trip in Aberdeen Bay, with a good complement of passengers. She is fitted with no less than four auxiliary sails. She was a Royal Navy minesweeper from 1914 to 1920, and was lost in collision with a German trawler on 12 May 1929. (Photo Aberdeen Museum).*

crew of eight, under Skipper George Warman, had time to launch their smallboat and get clear of their ship before she sank. The crew were picked up and taken to Aberdeen by the *Hede Sprenger*, which also towed in the *Loch Esk's* smallboat. The *Hede Sprenger* had been, from 1921 to 1923, the Aberdeen trawler *Star of Erin* (A 813), owned by Andrew Walker, later of the Walker steam Trawl Fishing Co. Ltd. She was one of five German trawlers built during the war which were bought by Walkers and given "Star" names, and all were sold back to Germany in 1923.

5 January 1930   *Braconmoor* (2)   A 767
194 Tons/1917

The *Braconmoor* was built for the Admiralty by Hall Russells as the *Samuel Baker*, and was bought on her release from the Navy by the Don Fishing Co. Ltd. of Aberdeen, along with three similar trawlers. All were given "Bracon" names, the others becoming *Braconash*, *Braconburn* and *Braconbush*.

The *Braconmoor* had sailed from Aberdeen on the Saturday morning, 4th January for the fishing grounds west of Orkney. By the early hours of Sunday she was at the western end of the Pentland Firth when she was enveloped in a rain squall at 12.45 am and struck a reef just off Torness, at the south-west corner of the Island of Hoy in Orkney. A heavy sea was running in this exposed place, and the crew sounded the ship's siren and fired off rockets to attract attention. The Longhope lifeboat was immediately launched to go to her aid, but in the heavy surf and strong tide, was unable to get close to the wreck. The lifeboatmen put out an anchor in an attempt to get closer, but failed to find a holding bottom. Eventually, at 4 am, the lifeboatmen succeeded in firing a line over the *Braconmoor* and were able to rig their life-saving apparatus and haul the nine crewmen one by one through the surf to the lifeboat. The crewmen were underwater practically all the time of the passage between wreck and lifeboat, and as the last man, Skipper Archie Brown, of Glenbervie Road, Torry, was being

hauled across, the breeches buoy turned upside down and he appeared to be unconscious when he reached the lifeboat. Artificial respiration was applied all the way to Longhope, but the skipper, who had commanded the *Braconmoor* for five years, was found to be dead. He left a widow and a grown-up daughter.

28 March 1930   *Ben Doran*   A 178   155 Tons/1900

Like her sister, the *Ben Rinnes*, lost almost exactly two years earlier, the *Ben Doran* was a Hall Russell ship, built for the North British Steam Fishing Co. Ltd, later Richard Irvin & Sons Ltd, sold in 1912 to Thomas Davidson of Aberdeen, and then in 1922 to John Lewis Ltd. and others. The "others" at the time of her loss were her skipper, James Caie of 4 Woodstock Road, Aberdeen and his father. Skipper Caie had served for seven years on the *Ben Doran*, the last two as master.

The *Ben Doran* was what was called at the time a Sunday boat, meaning that she never fished on a Sunday. If it was not practical to arrange for a landing in Aberdeen on the Saturday, the skipper would often call at Scalloway, on the west coast of Shetland, for the weekend, so that most of his crew became well-known to the people of Scalloway, indeed Skipper Caie often took an active part in the services at Scalloway Methodist Church. Late on the Friday night, 28th March, the *Ben Doran* was apparently making for Scalloway in poor visibility and a fresh south-west wind when she ran on to the Ve Skerries, some four miles north-west of the island of Papa Stour and twelve miles south-west of Hillswick, on the Shetland mainland. The skerries are a jagged mass of rocks, the highest point of which is only twelve feet above sea level, so that in even a moderate sea they are a mass of broken water. The time of the disaster must have been late in the evening, as a woman in Sandness saw, at 11.45 pm, what she took to be a chimney fire in a distant croft. It later transpired that there was no such fire, so what she had seen must have been the flares from the *Ben Doran*. The plight of the *Ben Doran* and her crew was first discovered by the Aberdeen trawler *Braconbush* (A 770) (a sister of the *Braconmoor* lost in January) at midday on the Saturday. Skipper Tom Wright immediately made for Hillswick and reported it to the coastguard in Lerwick. At the time there was no lifeboat station in Shetland, so the lifesaving apparatus and crew were called out at 5 pm and taken by road to the township of Heylor, a few miles from Hillswick, where they were loaded on to the Aberdeen trawler *Arora* (A 320) (Skipper Burnett). The darkness and an increasing wind forced the rescue effort to be held over till first light the next morning.

Mr. George Kay, a Lerwick man who had been appointed Honorary Secretary of the then anticipated Lerwick lifeboat and an experienced yachtsman, thought that a boat smaller than a trawler might be more successful in a rescue attempt. He, therefore, made for the village of Voe by car, and contacted Skipper John Jamieson of the Burra Isle haddock boat *Smiling Morn*, who with his three crew were most willing to make the attempt. They sailed as soon as they were able to borrow a small dinghy locally, and called in at Papa Stour, where they were able to get the services of Mr. John Henderson, who knew the Ve Skerries intimately. The *Smiling Morn* and the *Arora* arrived at the scene of the wreck as daylight came, and the smaller boat approached to within 400 yards of the wreck, close enough to identify the trawler by her number. The whole area was a solid mass of breaking water, making it quite impossible to go any closer. The *Ben Doran's* wheelhouse had gone, and seven men were clinging to the rigging of the foremast, the ones lower down being dressed in oilskins, and the upper ones in blue jerseys. By this time there were some nine fishing vessels at the scene including several Peterhead drifters, all quite unable to get any closer to be of assistance to the men. The crew of the *Smiling Morn* were convinced that the men were all alive at this time, as their heads were erect and turned to follow the boats as they steamed past. The *Arora* also could not get close enough for the lifesaving crew to be able to fire a rocket over the *Ben Doran*, so the boats at the scene had reluctantly to return to harbour.

The Stromness lifeboat under Coxswain William Linklater was called out on the Sunday afternoon, having stood by since late on Saturday afternoon, and arrived at Scalloway at 7.30 am on the Monday morning to refuel and take on a local pilot. By now the wind had moderated considerably, but on arriving at the Ve Skerries the lifeboatmen found that the *Ben Doran* had broken up. Watchers on Papa Stour reported that the foremast was seen to fall about midday on the Sunday, effectively ending the ordeal of the men still clinging to it.

The crew and their dependants were:-

James Caie, Skipper, 4 Woodstock Road — Widow and young family.
Peter Geddes, Mate, 23 Brimmond Place — Widow and three of a family.
William Skinner, Ch. Engineer, 21 South Constitution Street — Widow and two children.
Gilbert Watt, Sec. Engineer, 1 Hunter Place — Widower. No family.
William Christie, Fireman 88 Albion Street — Widow and grown-up children.
William Insh, Sec. Fisherman, 31 Park Road — Widow and four children.
Joseph Cormack, Deckhand, Seaman's Mission, Palmerston Road — Widow.
James Mitchell, Deckhand, 8 John Street — Widow. No family.
Henry Holgate, Cook, 5 Jopps Lane — Widow and four of a family.

About a month after the tragedy the bodies of two of the crew were found washed up on one of the skerries. One of them had a rope tied round his waist and attached to this was a long rope leading towards the wreck. The bodies were identified as those of William Insh and Joseph Cormack, who were both known as strong swimmers, and it appeared, since there were only seven men in the rigging on the Sunday that Insh and Cormack had attempted to get a rope ashore before the sea got up so heavily, and had died in the attempt. They were buried in adjoining graves in Sandness Kirkyard, under a

Memorial Stone, Ben Doran – The stone erected by public subscription in Sandness Kirkyard, Shetland to mark the graves of two crewmen from the **Ben Doran**, lost with her crew of nine on the Ve Skerries on 28 March 1930. The bodies of the two men, both strong swimmers, were found with a rope leading towards the wreck and they were presumed to have died in an attempt to bring their shipmates to the relative safety of the rocks. Second Fisherman Insh left a widow and four of a family. Deckhand Joseph Cormack had been married for only eight days. The grave is still tended by people in Shetland. (Photo Robert Johnson, Scalloway.)

Smiling Morn – The Shetland fishing boat **Smiling Morn** which was involved in a gallant but unavailing attempt to rescue the crew of the **Ben Doran**, stranded on the Ve Skerries on 28 March 1930. (Photo Shetland Museum).

memorial erected by friends in Shetland.

Cormack, a native of Portgordon, was only twenty-two years of age and had been married for only eight days. William Insh had gained his mate's certificate only two weeks previously.

The tragedy of the *Ben Doran* is still vividly remembered in Aberdeen and especially in Shetland, and caused such horror at the time that several steps were taken to ease the burdens of mariners in the area. The RNLI had already decided to station a lifeboat at Lerwick, but then decided to station one at Aith on the west side, so that the west coast would be more adequately covered. In addition, a flashing buoy was established close to the Ve Skerries. The Aberdeen motor trawler *Elinor Viking* (A 278) ran onto the Ve Skerries in December 1977 in a force 10 gale. Skipper Alex Flett radioed for assistance and he and his crew of seven were rescued under very severe and difficult conditions by a British Airways helicopter (Capt. George Bain) from Sumburgh.

A small automatic lighthouse was established on the skerries some years ago to provide greater safety cover for the tanker traffic to Sullom Voe.

25 April 1930   George Aunger   A 37   260 Tons/1918

The *George Aunger* was another Admiralty-built trawler, which was sold by the Navy in 1922 and retained her original name. She had been bought from Grimsby owners in June 1929 by George Leiper of Aberdeen and was on a coaling trip with six of a crew when she ran ashore on May Island, at the entrance to the Firth of Forth, in dense fog. Heavy seas were running and the six crewmen crowded into the wheelhouse for shelter. Within minutes the ship was struck by a huge wave which turned the trawler on her side and Skipper James Morrice of 145 Victoria Road, was thrown through the wheelhouse windows and washed away. The others now had to cling to the railings of the wheelhouse verandah as they were prevented by the surging waves from reaching the foremast and taking to the rigging. Some five hours after the ship struck, with the survivors well-nigh

exhausted with clinging in their precarious position, the fireman, W. Guyan, 26 Charles Street, a man of twenty-nine with a family of four who joined the crew at the last minute when another crewman did not turn up, lost his hold on the railings and he too was washed away. Shortly after this some lighthouse keepers came on the scene and as the tide was now ebbing, were able to clamber over rocks at the foot of the cliff and get a line aboard the stricken trawler. By means of ropes they were able to get the four survivors ashore, but the crewmen were so exhausted by their ordeal that they had practically to be carried to the lighthouse buildings.

The Aberdeen trawler *Ethel Crawford* (A 36) (q.v.) had run ashore on May Island just five weeks earlier on 22nd March, fortunately without loss of life, and was successfully refloated after some weeks. The *George Aunger*, however, became a total loss.

30 April 1930   Ben Lawers   A 311   176 Tons/1900

The *Ben Lawers* was one of six trawlers built in 1900 for the North British Steam Fishing Co. Ltd, later Richard Irvin & Sons Ltd, and had been sold to J. Craig, Aberdeen in 1917 while still requisitioned as a minesweeper. On the day of her loss she had left Aberdeen in the afternoon on a North Sea fishing trip and shortly afterwards ran into thick fog. Speed was reduced and she was groping her way through the fog when with a loud crash, the Hull trawler *St Neots* (H 112), crashed into her, damaging her so severely that she immediately began to sink. The Hull skipper had the presence of mind to keep his ship's engines turning ahead to keep his ship's bow in the hole in the *Ben Lawers*. The *Ben Lawers'* crew of nine, under Skipper J. Strachan, 15 Ferry Road, Torry, were able to climb on to the whaleback of the *St. Neots* before their ship slid to the bottom, only minutes after the impact. The *St. Neots* brought the shipwrecked crew to Aberdeen.

21 January 1931   Cransdale   A 453   183 Tons/1901

The *Cransdale* was returning to Aberdeen from a fishing trip when she grounded on the Outers, off St.

Fergus, in fog. Her distress flares were answered by both the Peterhead lifeboat, under Coxswain James Strachan, and the Peterhead lifesaving apparatus. The lifeboat was first on the scene, and succeeded in getting alongside the *Cransdale*, rescuing Skipper Alex King and his eight crew members and bringing them safely to Peterhead. The lifeboat then returned to the wreck and found the *Cransdale* afloat. A towline was put on board and the lifeboat took the *Cransdale* in tow, hoping to get her to the safety of Peterhead harbour. After one and a half hours of towing, however, the *Cransdale* was seen to be in a sinking condition and finally foundered in seventeen fathoms of water.

The *Cransdale* was formerly named *Harry Ross*, one of three trawlers built simultaneously by Hall Russell for the Ross Steam Trawling & Fishing Co. Ltd. and called after members of the family. The *Maggie Ross* and *Jane Ross* were both also lost at sea, the former being captured by a U-Boat in 1917 and the latter being wrecked at Crail on the Fife coast in 1934.

6 July 1931   *Raindrop*   A 434   167 Tons/1912

The *Raindrop*, under Skipper/owner James Wood, 22 Devanha Gardens, and his eight crewmen, sailed from Aberdeen at six o'clock on the Monday morning, 6th July, for the fishing grounds and shortly afterwards ran into dense fog. Speed was reduced and an extra lookout kept. At 8.30 am, when she was only some ten miles from Aberdeen, she was in collision with the steam coaster *Rydal Force* of Whitehaven, on a voyage to Newcastle. The little *Raindrop* was severely damaged, and the Master of the *Rydal Force*, like the skipper of the *St. Neots* in similar circumstances the previous year when he collided with the *Ben Lawers*, kept his ship in the hole in the *Raindrop's* side to give the trawlermen time to launch their smallboat. They succeeded in getting the boat into the water and had just pulled away to go alongside the coaster when a figure appeared on the *Raindrop's* deck, waving and shouting to his companions to wait. It was the Chief Engineer, D. Cheyne, who had gone below for

something after the order to man the smallboat was given. He was just able to scramble into the boat when the *Raindrop* sank, only eight minutes after the collision. The nine crewmen were taken aboard the *Rydal Force* whose master proposed taking them to Newcastle, his ship's destination. Skipper Wood explained, however, that they were no distance from Aberdeen and suggested that if the ship were to close the land, they might come across a local trawler which could land them in Aberdeen. The Aberdeen trawler *Sanserit* (A 404) was sighted afterwards, and as she was making for Aberdeen with her catch of fish, the coaster's boat was launched (presumably the *Raindrop's* boat had not been retained by the *Rydal Force* but had been left to drift) and the *Sanserit* brought the nine survivors to Aberdeen, arriving about midday, only six hours after the *Raindrop* had sailed.

Two other Aberdeen trawlers, the *Strathallan* (A 954) and the *Avondow* (A 56), collided in fog just off Aberdeen at 9 am that morning. Both of them were damaged and returned to port.

20 July 1931   *Sanguine*   A 359   204 Tons/1918

This oddly-named trawler (her previous name had been *Claribelle* when she had been brought to Aberdeen three years previously) was making for the fishing grounds north of Shetland when she ran on to the Little Rumble Rocks at the entrance to Yell Sound, Shetland at 4.45 in the afternoon. Lerwick lifeboat was called out, as was the Yell lifesaving crew which had to be brought from Burravoe in Yell on a motorboat. Skipper James Bruce, 188 Victoria Road, reported that his ship was not making water and that the crew would remain on board, but he put out a kedge anchor to enable the *Sanguine* to pull herself off the rocks and the lifeboat also assisted, but to no avail. The Admiralty diverted HMS *Dee*, a fishery patrol trawler which had been on patrol near Foula, to assist, and three drifters, *Ardlaw* (Buckie) *Cormorant* (Banff) and *Spes Melior* (Kirkcaldy) were engaged by the trawler's insurance company, but their combined efforts failed to budge the *Sanguine*. The powerful salvage tug *Bullger* of Leith arrived on 24th July, but found that nothing could be done and had to leave the *Sanguine* to the mercy of the fierce tides in that dangerous spot. The crew were taken off by Lerwick lifeboat.

27 August 1931   *Choice*   A 764   165 Tons/1905

The *Choice* had been sold to a Port Seton owner in 1930 and was carrying a crew of eight from the Edinburgh area. About 9 pm, while the trawler was fishing eighteen miles off Peterhead, the chief engineer reported that she was making water fast, apparently as a result of damage to one of her plates by a trawl door. In answer to her distress flare, the drifter *Copious* (KY 175) of Anstruther, came alongside and took off the crew. A towrope was rigged and the *Copious* began the tow to the nearest land, but after two hours the *Choice* heeled over and sank. The *Copious* landed the eight survivors in Anstruther.

25 September 1931   *Davan*   A 117   222 Tons/1909

The *Davan* was one of a pair of ex-Belgian trawlers bought by A.A. Davidson in 1930, the other being the *Ordie* (A 119), both being re-named after adjoining Aberdeenshire estates. The *Davan* ran ashore in fog at the foot of towering 1000 foot cliffs below Myggenaes Light in Faroe. In answer to the continuous sounding of the siren, one of the lighthouse keepers spotted the ship from the top of the cliffs, and lost no time in launching his own boat from the local small harbour and making for the *Davan*. The eight crew, including Skipper Gove, were able to launch their smallboat and row across to the motorboat, which took them to Myggenaes harbour. The Aberdeen salvage vessel *Henry Lancaster*, an ex-Admiralty trawler, was despatched to Faroe to try to salvage the *Davan*, but there was nothing she could do except to bring the survivors home to Aberdeen.

2 December 1931   *Nairn*   A 524   197 Tons/1910

The *Nairn* had been built by Duthies, Torry, in 1910 as the trawler *Driver*. She was purchased by the Admiralty in 1910 for use as a minesweeping training ship to train crews of the fishery reserve which later became the nucleus of the Auxiliary Patrol during World War 1. It is interesting that the Admiralty had paid little attention to mine warfare up to this time, and that even at the outbreak of war in August 1914 the total minesweeping force of the Royal Navy amounted only to ten old converted torpedo gunboats and thirteen trawlers, of which the *Driver* was one. She had been re-named *Nairn* by the Navy in 1919 and retained that name when sold in 1920.

About 11 pm, in pitch darkness and in the teeth of a seventy-mile-an-hour south-easterly gale, the *Nairn* was making for Aberdeen after a short fishing trip when she drove on to rocks about 100 yards offshore from 150-foot cliffs at Broadhaven, one mile south of Collieston. Her distress flares were seen immediately by Coastguard Sullivan, who was on bad weather watch at Collieston coastguard station and who now advised the Peterhead and Aberdeen lifeboat stations and called out the Collieston life-saving brigade. The rocket apparatus had to be dragged for a mile over sand dunes and marshy ground to the wreck, the rocket brigade being willingly assisted by every able-bodied man in the village, and shortly after midnight the gear was assembled on the clifftop above the wreck. After three attempts to fire a rocket line over the trawler had been thwarted by the furious gale, it was decided to move the apparatus to the foot of the cliff. In the flickering light of flares and lanterns this was a daunting and dangerous task, but, at last, the apparatus was again assembled and at the second attempt a rocket line was connected to the trawler. After some difficulty with a fouled whip block the breeches buoy was rigged up and the crew of ten were hauled to safety one by one, the last man ashore being Skipper Hugh Greig of 26 Castle Terrace. A newspaper reporter on the scene recorded that the survivors were met at the clifftop by the women of the village, who provided them (and presumably the rescuers) with "pails of steaming hot tea".

The Aberdeen lifeboat had meantime arrived nearby, but was unable to approach the wreck in the fury of the storm, and stood by offshore. When the last man was safely ashore the coastguards signalled the "all-clear" to the lifeboat, the *Emma Constance*, and she returned to Aberdeen.

29 April 1932 *Braconash* A 728 212 Tons/1918

The *Braconash* had been built by Alexander Hall & Co. of Aberdeen for the Admiralty as the *John Clay* and was on loan to the U.S. Navy for a period before being sold by the Admiralty to Councillor J.S. Doig of Aberdeen in 1921.

She had sailed from Aberdeen with nine of a crew under Skipper Alex Flockhart, 47 Glenbervie Road, on a Friday afternoon. The fog at the time was very dense, and she had gone only five or six miles from the port when she was in collision with the Aberdeen trawler *Strathlethen* (A 948). She was badly holed amidships, so the skipper ordered the smallboat to be launched and the crew rowed to the *Strathlethen* which was standing by, although they could barely see her in the dense fog. The *Strathlethen* stood by for some hours before bringing the crew of the *Braconash* back to Aberdeen.

The Aberdeen trawler *Devanha* (A 458) was in collision with the Grimsby trawler *Lord Beaconsfield* in the fog three miles off Buchan Ness later that day. The *Devanha's* bows were damaged, but she was able to reach Aberdeen. At about the same time, an unknown trawler ran on to the rocks at Gadle Braes, Peterhead. Peterhead lifeboat and the life-saving brigade made for the scene, but the trawler succeeded in refloating herself and their services were not required.

2 September 1932 *Strathmiglo* A 163 203 Tons/1918

Unlike most of the Strath fleet of trawlers, which had been built for the Aberdeen Steam Trawling & Fishing Co. Ltd. by Hall Russell of Aberdeen, the *Strathmiglo* had been built by Hawthorns of Leith as the Admiralty trawler *Henry Harding*. Sold by the Admiralty in 1920, she became the *Ocean Clipper* of Yarmouth, and arrived in Aberdeen in 1926 under that name, being re-named *Strathmiglo* in 1927.

At 11 pm on the day of her loss she was in collision six miles off Strathy Point, Caithness with the Danish steamer *Kristen*, a ship of 3000 tons bound from Glasgow to Copenhagen with a cargo of coke. The *Strathmiglo* was struck admidships, and her engine room rapidly filled with water. The two vessels remained locked for a short time, sufficient for the nine trawlermen, including Skipper Peter Henderson, to clamber up the side of the *Kristen* to her deck. The *Kristen* landed the men at Thurso and proceeded on her voyage, the only damage being to her stem.

2 January 1933 *Venetia* A 560 201 Tons/1899

The *Venetia* was built at Beverley and bought second-hand from Grimsby in 1922 by the Walker Steam Trawl Fishing Co. of Aberdeen, who in turn sold her in November 1932, less than two months before her loss, to her skipper, Alex Wood (37) of Clifton Road, Aberdeen, and trawlowner George R. Wood of North Esplanade East. Most of Aberdeen's trawling fleet made a point of being home for a few days over the New Year, but Skipper Wood would have been anxious to get in an extra trip over the New Year when fish landings were invariably low and would fetch a good price at the market.

On the Thursday before New Year (29th December) he sailed from Aberdeen with his usual crew of nine, including two brothers of his wife, David (35) and James Lovie (43), both of whom lived with the skipper and his wife in Clifton Road. Skipper Wood had not advised his co-owner where he intended fishing, but this was normal practice, and he had said that he intended to be back in Aberdeen on the following Tuesday (3rd January), for the first market of the year.

On the Sunday evening, New Year's Day, Coastguard Brokenshire of Stonehaven went on duty at the lookout station at 8 pm. It was a fine night until 10 o'clock, with

Sanguine – The **Sanguine** *(A 359) aground on the Rumble Rocks, Yell Sound, Shetland, after grounding there on 20 July 1931. This photograph must have been taken some months later, judging by the seabird droppings on her side, but her trawl net still hangs from her funnel and the trawl door is still stowed beside the forward gallows. (Photo Shetland Museum).*

Ben Screel – The **Ben Screel** *(A 121) on the rocks beside Girdleness Lighthouse, Aberdeen, after running ashore in thick fog on 18 January 1933. Her crew of ten were rescued by Life-Saving Apparatus. (Photo George Coull Collection).*

the moon shining and the stars out, and there was nothing unusual to note. The moon set about 10 o'clock and a change came over the weather; the wind increased in strength and the visibility decreased. Around half an hour earlier, Brokenshire had observed the lights of the local steamer *Locksley* as she arrived off Stonehaven with a cargo of coal and dropped anchor to await the tide to enter the harbour. He kept her lights under observation, knowing that if the wind were to increase to gale force from the south there would be a great risk of her going on to the Brachans, a grim area of jagged rocks in Stonehaven Bay, visible only at low water.

At 1.15 am Brokenshire telephoned his relief, Coastguard John Clarke, who was due to take over his watch at the lookout hut at 2 am. About twenty minutes before Clarke arrived, Brokenshire spotted the lights of a trawler abreast of the hut and about four miles out to sea. Clarke in his turn kept both ships under observation, and noticed that the trawler was now burning additional lights, from which he deduced that the ship had hauled up her trawl and the crew were sorting the catch before lowering the trawl again. The weather, meantime, had worsened considerably and by 2.30 am it was blowing a full gale from the south with visibility closed down to about half a mile. Just after this a blizzard of driving rain and sleet struck, reducing visibility to such an extent that Clarke was unable to see even the breakers beneath his hut. The squall continued for about half an hour, when visibility increased to about two miles. He saw no further sign of the trawler before his relief arrived at 8 am.

About 10.30 in the forenoon, a farm servant from the farm of Auquhorthies, Isaac Spark, was working in one of the fields at the clifftop when he spotted a trawler well up on the rocks at the foot of the 100 foot high cliffs at Holehead, about a mile north of the coastguard hut. He could make out the name and number of the trawler —*Venetia* (A 560) — but there was no sign of life and a mass of wreckage littered the foreshore. He ran to the farm, some three fields distant, and his employer, Mr. Alan Blacklaws, hurried to the police office in Stonehaven to report the tragedy. The Coastguards and the lifeboat secretary were immediately informed, and the rocket gun at the harbour called out the lifeboat crew. With the day being a public holiday, most Stonehaven people were at home, so the explosion of the lifeboat maroon brought large crowds to the harbour to watch the launch. It was a hazardous job to get the lifeboat into the water from its large four-wheeled carriage, and the fact that some of the crew were still sleeping off their New Year celebrations led to Coxswain William King having to make up his crew with two young men volunteers. The Lifeboat, *Joseph Ridgway*, was a pulling and sailing boat with no engine, and with the mountainous seas now running at the harbour mouth there were tense moments as the watching crowd saw the boat crawl her way slowly out from the relative safety of the harbour to the open sea. The Coastguards meantime had brought out their rocket apparatus and life-saving equipment, hitched to a motor lorry, and this set off for the wreck. Due, apparently, to a confusion in names, both lifeboat and apparatus had been directed southwards to Tod Head, six miles south of Stonehaven, instead of to Holehead, three miles north. A local news reporter ran to hire a taxi, one of the very few in Stonehaven at the time, and set off in pursuit of the rocket apparatus, which was by now well ahead of him. As he approached the road to Crawton, some four miles south, he and his driver recognised the wheel tracks of the apparatus on the Crawton road, but on reaching the Crawton farm at the end of the road the apparatus was nowhere to be seen. They doubled back and took a short cut to the village of Catterline, where they learned that there was no wreck in the vicinity and that the apparatus had gone back to Stonehaven. On the way back, they met hundreds of people hurrying southwards in the face of a terrific rainstorm, while hundreds more could be seen hurrying along the clifftop path towards Dunnottar Castle in the hope of spotting the wreck.

In the meantime, the lifeboat coxswain had realised that, in such a sea and with his boat's severe limitations in manoeuvring, there would be no possibility of approaching a wreck which was aground, so with great difficulty he succeeded in turning his boat round and making his way back to harbour. The Aberdeen lifeboat had also put to sea in the hope of effecting a rescue, but was recalled by radio when coastguards had advised that she would be unable to be of assistance.

By early afternoon, large crowds had made their way to the clifftop above the wreck, much to the surprise of the occupants of a farm only a few hundred yards from the scene, who were quite unaware of what had happened almost on their doorstep. By this time the *Venetia* had been completely broken up, and a mass of shattered timber washed into an inlet at the foot of the cliffs, together with lifebelts bearing the ship's name, was all that was visible.

With the aid of ropes, Inspector Thom and other officers of Stonehaven police, coastguards and other helpers, made their way down the steep cliffs in an effort to recover some of the bodies, which could be seen being tossed about by the breakers, but these were repeatedly carried away by the backwash and only two were later recovered. The only woman to venture down the cliffs was Miss Mitchell, daughter of a Stonehaven iron-monger, who had arrived with rugs and blankets in the hope of rendering assistance.

A tragic figure near the scene was Mrs. Wood, wife of the skipper, who had gone to the fish market earlier in the day in the hope of greeting her husband and her two brothers on their return from their fishing trip, and had heard that a trawler had gone ashore. She was driven by a friend to the scene of the disaster, and remained at the roadside in the car, but no-one would take it upon himself to tell her either the name of the trawler or the fate of the crew. The sad news was broken to her only later. One of her brothers, James, the fireman on the *Venetia*, had returned to Aberdeen only the previous year after twenty years in Australia, and he was on only his second trip on the *Venetia*.

The *Venetia's* crew were:-

Skipper: Alexander Wood (37)	500 Clifton Road
Mate: Alexander Noble (32)	7 Tanfield Walk
Sec.Fisherman: Robert Cran (36)	50 School Road
Ch.Engineer: David Pirie (62)	53 Upperkirkgate
Sec.Engineer: David Lovie (35)	c/o 500 Clifton Road
Fireman: James Lovie (43)	c/o 500 Clifton Road
Deckhand: Andrew Wood (60)	33 Menzies Road
Deckhand: John Morrice (33)	54 School Drive
Cook: C. Morgan (43)	72 Tullos Crescent

18 January 1933   *Ben Screel*   A 121   197 Tons/1914

The *Ben Screel*, one of Richard Irvin & Sons famous Ben Line of trawlers, was homeward bound from a fishing trip and was nearing the harbour entrance in thick fog when Skipper Henry Bowman, 34 Middlefield Terrace, realised from the sound of the Girdleness foghorn that he was about half a mile south of the entrance. He made to turn the ship northwards when she took the rocks just below the lighthouse and remained fast. The continuous sounding of the siren brought to the scene Robert Law, a corporation sewage plant attendant, whose premises were at Girdleness, and who now clambered over the rocks to shout "Dinna worry, boys! Stand by for the lifeline." The Girdleness lighthouse keepers alerted the lifesaving brigades and both the Torry harbour and the Aberdeen brigades turned out. By now six of the crew were in the foremast rigging with the remaining four in the wheelhouse, and the *Ben Screel* was being pounded by heavy seas. The Torry brigade sent their first rocket over the ship's stern, a place too dangerous for the trawlermen to recover the line, but their second one was more accurate and the men were able to haul out the breeches buoy hawser and make it fast. This rope however was fouled and the breeches buoy could not be operated. While the rescuers struggled to clear the buoy, one of the *Ben Screel's* crew, second engineer Edwin Taylor of China Cottage, St. Fitticks Road, came ashore hand over hand on the rope and fell into the hands of the rescuers on the rocks. Until

51

then the name of the ship was not known, so dense was the fog. Taylor's brother, David, was a fireman on the trawler, and he and the rest of the crew were brought ashore in the breeches buoy, several of them only scantily clad and in an exhausted state. Two of them were taken to hospital for treatment, as was a coastguard who had been swept off his feet by a wave and dashed on the rocks.

18 January 1933   *Struan*   A 718   213 Tons/1918

Later the same evening the *Struan*, a former Strath class Admiralty trawler built by Alexander Hall in 1918 and named *William Cogswell*, ran ashore in fog about 10 pm on the Outers, a range of rocks off Scotstoun Head, south of Rattray Head lighthouse. The alarm was raised by two young men, who had heard the trawler's siren, and Peterhead lifeboat, under Coxswain John Strachan, and the Peterhead life saving brigade, were called out. The brigade had some difficulty in reaching the scene as they were faced with the Herculean task of transporting their gear over sand dunes for over a mile after leaving the road. Having set up their apparatus, their first rocket fell wide of the *Struan*, but their second was on target and the trawlermen began to pull in the line. However, the lifeboat had just succeeded in getting alongside the trawler after six attempts and quickly took off the nine crewmen, including Skipper William Shepherd of 173 Great Northern Road, Aberdeen. The rocket brigade were not aware for some time that the crew had been rescued by the lifeboat as the visibility was so poor, but eventually it became clear that there was no further need for their service. Weary and frustrated, they made their way back to Peterhead.

27 February 1933   *Avondow*   A 56   197 Tons/1914

The *Avondow* had been built in Aberdeen for Hartlepool owners as the *Miriam Stewart* (HL 10) and was purchased from Scarborough owners in 1924 by the North Star Steam Fishing Co. Ltd. and renamed *Avondow* in 1925. She was on a fishing trip to Orkney waters under Skipper Alex Flett when she was forced to shelter from a south-easterly gale in Lashy Sound, between the Orkney islands of Sanday and Eday. She foundered at Millgoe, but the ten crewmen managed to launch their smallboat and row across the Sound to land safely on Eday.

5 May 1933   *Florence Dombey*   A 264   182 Tons/1900

The *Florence Dombey* was an old trawler which had been bought from Fleetwood in 1920. She had been taken over by the Navy as a boom defence vessel in 1915, but had been released to go back to fishing in 1918, presumably because of her advancing years. Now fifteen years later she was fishing out of Aberdeen, under Skipper Jack Hague, 50 Ruthrieston Circle, with a crew of ten, including a boy. After calling at Granton, the *Florence Dombey* set out for the fishing grounds off the Longstone Light and had just arrived when the Chief Engineer discovered that water was rushing in through the main bunkers. The pumps were immediately started but were powerless to cope with the inflow. Fortunately, the Aberdeen trawler *Arora* (A 320) (which had been involved with the attempted rescue of the *Ben Doran's* crew three years earlier) was fishing nearby, and she came alongside to enable the eleven crewmen to scramble aboard. The *Florence Dombey* sank only thirty-five minutes from the time the leak was discovered. One of the crew, who had been asleep in his bunk, left the ship clad only in his underwear, while the skipper had no time to go to his cabin to collect his false teeth before he had to jump for his life. The *Arora* brought the *Florence Dombey's* crew to Anstruther, where they arrived in the early hours of the morning. According to a newspaper report "The local policeman was roused, and the wrecked crew were put up at a boarding house for the night."

28 June 1933   *Strathurie*   A 403   210 Tons/1911

The *Strathurie* was built by Hall Russell for the Strath fleet of the Aberdeen Steam Trawling & Fishing Co. Ltd. and was one of the first trawlers to be taken up by the

Avondow – The *Avondow* (A 122), built in 1946, was the last steam trawler fishing from Aberdeen when she finally went to the scrapyard in Bo'ness in September 1967. She is seen here setting out on a fishing trip from Aberdeen. (Photo George Coull Collection).

Margaret Clark – The *Margaret Clark* about to sail on her trip in 1929. She was wrecked at Iceland on a fishing trip four years later on 10 December 1933. (Photo Aberdeen Museum).

Royal Navy at the commencement of World War 1 in August 1914. Returned in 1919, she fished for her owners till 1929, when she was sold to T.H. Scales, the Newhaven trawlowner, in 1929. Like the *Florence Dombey* the previous month, the *Strathurie* sprang a leak while fishing off the Longstone Light and began to founder. Her crew, presumably from the Edinburgh area as no names were given in the Aberdeen newspapers, took to their smallboat and were afloat in it for several hours before being picked up by the Hull trawler *Cape Matapan* (H 238) (later to be an Aberdeen trawler in 1946 with the registration A 80) and landed at Hull.

10 December 1933   *Margaret Clark*   A 1
288 Tons/1929

The *Margaret Clark* was one of Aberdeen's larger and newer trawlers built in 1929 by Hall Russell for the Nairn Fishing Co. Ltd. of Aberdeen. While on a fishing trip to Iceland, she ran ashore at Oeraefi. The German trawler *Konsul Dubbers* launched her boat, manned by all six deckhands in her crew, to go to the rescue but the boat was overturned in the heavy surf and two of the would-be rescuers were drowned. The four others, as well as the whole crew of the *Margaret Clark* with Skipper John Clark, were rescued by Icelanders.

Skipper Clark was in command of HMT *Robert Bowen* when she was bombed and sunk by German aircraft off Aberdeen on 9th February 1940, while in company with HMT *Fort Royal*. Skipper Clark was killed, as were all of his crew.

16 January 1934   *Loch Ard* (2)   A 151   351 Tons/1931

The *Loch Ard* had been built by John Lewis & Sons Ltd. for the Loch Line Steam Fishing Co. Ltd. of Aberdeen and Hull. She left Hull for a voyage to the Iceland fishing grounds and was never seen again after she had called in at Aberdeen on her way north. Of her crew of thirteen, twelve came from Hull and one from Aberdeen.

6 March 1934   *Victory*   A 692   164 Tons/1898

One of Aberdeen's oldest trawlers — even the Navy had only retained her for nine months, probably on account of her age at that time — the *Victory* was on a coaling trip to the Firth of Forth with a full crew of nine men, including Skipper John D. Buchan Jnr, 8 Walker Road and the mate John D. Buchan Sen. of the same address. At 8 pm, in dense fog, she grounded at the north end of the Isle of May, at the entrance to the Firth of Forth. Flares were fired off and her siren sounded, and in answer to these, Anstruther lifeboat was launched. The *Victory* had been badly holed and within two hours was filled with water. Before the lifeboat could reach the scene, the Anstruther fishing boat *Enterprise* located the *Victory* and, in spite of a choppy sea, succeeded in getting near enough the wreck for the nine crewmen to jump to safety. The *Enterprise* brought the crew to Anstruther.

7 April 1934   *Mansfield*   A 685   165 Tons/1897

Like the *Victory* just a month earlier the *Mansfield* was a tired old trawler bought from Grimsby in 1921. In 1929 she had been sold to Ritchie and Davies, a Milford Haven firm, but had retained her Aberdeen registration although she was now fishing from Milford Haven with a local crew. She foundered twenty miles from the Coningbeg Light Vessel off the coast of Ireland. Her crew were picked up by the trawler *Peterborough* (HL 41), also owned in Milford Haven though registered in Hartlepool, and landed in Milford.

14 September 1934   *Jane Ross*   A 454   184 Tons/1901

The *Jane Ross* was the last survivor of the three trawlers built in Aberdeen in 1901 for the Ross Steam Trawling & Fishing Co. Ltd. and given family names. A further two were built in 1903 by the Smiths Dock Ltd. in North Shields, but were sold to France in 1905. *Jane Ross* had changed owners three times since the war. With her full crew of nine on board, under Skipper William Wemyss, 10 Ashvale Place, she was making for Methil for bunker coal in thick fog when she grounded at

Kilminning Point, two miles from Crail on the Fife coast. In response to her distress signals, Skipper Robert Murray of the Crail fishing boat *Maypole* succeeded in bringing his boat alongside the *Jane Ross* and rescuing the nine trawlermen, who were landed safely at Crail.

19 September 1934   *Avonglen*   A 137   208 Tons/1905

The *Avonglen* was previously the *Gillygate* (LO 231), bought in 1925 by J.A. Harrow along with her sister *Fishergate* (LO 209), which he re-named *Avondon* (A 136). Both were built by Smiths Dock Co. Ltd., North Shields. At the time of her loss the *Avonglen* was owned by the North Star Steam Fishing Co. Ltd. and her master was Skipper James Watson, 9 Grampian Circle. She was a "Sunday Boat", i.e. never fishing on a Sunday, and had left Aberdeen on the Monday forenoon for a week's fishing.

On the Tuesday night she was fishing in a half gale and a rising sea 105 miles NE x N of Buchan Ness. At 11 pm, when the crew were hauling in the trawl, the chief engineer reported a leak in the engine room. The pumps were immediately started up and as soon as the trawl doors were aboard, Skipper Watson steamed his ship over to the Aberdeen trawler *Beathwood* (A 442), which was fishing nearby, and asked her skipper to stand by. As the water was steadily rising in the *Avonglen*, it was decided to make for the nearest port, with the *Beathwood* in company. After half an hour's steaming the water had reached the engine room platform, and it was seen that it was hopeless to continue, so the smallboat was launched and the crew rowed over to the *Beathwood*. The *Beathwood* continued to stand by the stricken *Avonglen* until she finally sank eight hours later, and brought her crew back to Aberdeen.

15 March 1935   *Strathatholl*   A 477   209 Tons/1912

The *Strathatholl* had been one of the Aberdeen Steam Trawling & Fishing Co. Ltd.'s Strath fleet from her building by Hall Russell in 1912 until she was sold to private owners in 1930. Under Skipper Ben Buchan of 21

Whinnyfold, Cruden Bay, she was fishing twenty-five miles NE of Kinnaird Head when she sprang a leak. The pumps were unable to cope with the inrush of water, so the crew of ten took to the smallboat and stood by until their ship foundered. They rowed for sixteen hours before being picked up by the Norwegian steamer *Royksund*, which landed them in Thurso.

18 August 1935   *Gareloch*   A 276   246 Tons/1908

The *Gareloch* was formerly the *Lily Melling* (FD 222) of Fleetwood, and had been bought by W. Gove of Aberdeen in 1933 and re-named. She was returning to Aberdeen from a coaling trip to Methil with a crew of five when she ran ashore on rocks at Billowness, Anstruther. Four of her crew were able to walk over the rocks to safety, but engineer James Clark broke several ribs when the ship suddenly listed, and he had to be carried ashore by stretcher.

23 August 1935   *Port Jackson*   A 222   197 Tons/1904

Built by Duthies for Fleetwood owners in 1904, the *Port Jackson* was bought in November 1934 by the Regent Fishing Co. Ltd. and registered in Aberdeen. She was on a four-day fishing trip from Aberdeen and was moving to new grounds in heavy fog when she grounded on rocks at Scotstoun Head, north of Peterhead. About 3 am her distress flares and siren alerted Mr. J. Henderson, the coast lifesaving member at Scotstoun Head, who called out the life-saving brigade and Peterhead lifeboat. The brigade's new trailer soon reached the end of the metalled road to the scene, and was pulled from there to the beach by Mr. Henderson's horses. Just short of Scotstoun Head the trailer became stuck in the soft sand, so the brigade members had to carry the heavy gear themselves. It was then discovered that the *Port Jackson* was between 600 and 700 yards from the nearest point which the apparatus could reach. However, the lifeboat could by now be seen approaching, so the brigade took no further action.

In the meantime, Skipper Sam Bavidge Jun., 22

Port Jackson – The **Port Jackson** *(A 222) had been built in Aberdeen in 1904 for Fleetwood owners and was registered in Aberdeen for only a few months before she was wrecked north of Peterhead on 23 August 1935. In this photograph she is seen leaving Fleetwood on a fishing trip. (Photo George Coull Collection).*

George Stroud – *Minus her wheelhouse, in which three men were sheltering when it was carried away, the wreck of the* **George Stroud** *lies only yards from the North Pier at Aberdeen after her loss on 25 December 1935. The South Breakwater is in the background. (From a newspaper photograph – George Coull Collection).*

Claremont Street, had ordered the smallboat to be launched in case of emergency but had retained the crew on board in the hope that his ship could be towed off. As she continued to fill with water, however, the skipper decided to send five of his crew ashore in the lifeboat, which now came alongside and the men were taken off without difficulty. The remaining four took to the smallboat and stood by, but there was nothing they could do and the lifeboat had to return to the wreck, of which only the funnel was still visible, and bring the men to Peterhead.

26 August 1935 *Cassandra* A 236 174 Tons/1905

While fishing 46 miles ENE of Aberdeen the *Cassandra* sprang a leak and began to founder. Skipper William Geddes, 145 Victoria Road, ordered the smallboat to be launched and took to the boat with his eight crewmen shortly before the *Cassandra* sank. The nine men were picked up by the Peterhead drifter *Hopeful* (PD 504), which was on her way out on a herring trip, and were landed at Peterhead. One of the survivors, engineer Roderick McRae, 177 Spital, was to lose his life barely five years later when the trawler *Soar* was lost near Gourdon.

25 December 1935 *George Stroud* A 88
310 Tons/1930

The *George Stroud*, one of Aberdeen's largest and most modern trawlers, was returning from a coaling trip to Methil. Although it was Christmas Day, this was not a recognised holiday for the Aberdeen fishing community at that time and it was regarded as a normal working day. The fish market was open as usual and would be closed only on New Year's Day. It was a dark night, with a strong south-easterly wind, but it was not regarded as dangerous for the passage of ships up the harbour entrance channel, though caution was necessary as the wind was causing a nasty surge along the south edge of the north pier. At 8 pm the lookout on duty at the roundhouse at the landward end of the pier watched the

trawler's steaming lights as she slowly passed the south breakwater and shaped up for the channel. Suddenly, a huge stern sea struck the *George Stroud* and threw her well to starboard of her intended course. Before any corrective wheel action could take effect, the *George Stroud* crashed against the ledge of the pier and was swept bumping and grinding along the ledge until she came to a stop 200 yards from the seaward end of the pier, with a heavy list to starboard. The roundhouse lookout, horrified at the suddenness of the mishap, immediately called out the Footdee life-saving apparatus and telephoned harbour-master Captain Wyness, who was the lifeboat secretary, advising him that the lifeboat was required immediately. The lifeboat was on her way just seven minutes later and by the time she reached the wreck the life-saving brigade were already at the scene and were lifting a motor car on to the pier wall to provide light, as the trawler's lights had failed. Four men were sheltering in the trawler's wheelhouse but, although several rocket lines were fired, the men seemed reluctant or unable to go outside to make them fast. The small crowd of watchers on the pier heard repeatedly the cry "Send us the lifeboat". Meanwhile the lifeboat, under Coxswain Tom Sinclair, had been making repeated efforts to get alongside, and had got alongside the trawler's starboard side, between the ship and the pier, but the crew made no attempt to board her. The lifeboat by now had sustained damage to her side, and one of her propellers had been fouled by a rope, but despite this another attempt was made to get alongside, this time near the stern, as a red pinpoint of light had been spotted in the region of the ship's galley. This turned out to be from a cigarette held by the trawler's cook, Alex Wood of The Sailor's Home in Mearns Street. Lifelines were thrown in Wood's direction and the lifeboat crew waited as Wood came out of the galley and grasped one of the ropes. As he did so a wave crashed over and he had to retreat again to the galley, keeping a grip on the rope. As the wave passed he got to the ship's side, but then was struck by another wave and disappeared into the sea. In the forlorn hope that Wood was still clinging on, the lifeboatmen pulled in the rope, and to their relief Wood re-appeared above the water and was quickly helped aboard the lifeboat.

At about this time it was seen that the wooden upper part of the trawler's wheelhouse had been carried away and only one of the four men who had taken refuge in it was left clinging to the wrecked ironwork. He was bareheaded and clad only in a singlet and trousers. Slowly, as wave after wave threatened to sweep him away, he made his way down to the deck and grasped one of the rocket lines. He was able to make this fast and soon the breeches buoy was rigged and he was hauled on to the pier, where he was taken to a waiting car and rushed to the Infirmary. He turned out to be the second engineer, George Paterson of 7 Black's Buildings, Woolmanhill.

The lifeboat and life-saving apparatus remained at the scene for a further hour, until it became clear that there could be no more survivors. Skipper James Phillips, Mate A. Walker and Chief Engineer Tom Barras, all near neighbours from Victoria Road, had all perished, barely a mile from their homes.

18 January 1936   *Evergreen*   A 184   180 Tons/1902

The *Evergreen* was a Govan built trawler bought from Hull in November 1934 and owned by A. Bruce of Merkland Road East.

On her way home to Aberdeen from a fishing trip, the *Evergreen* grounded on the rocks in a blinding snowstorm about 1.45 am, between Rosehearty and Sandhaven on the north Aberdeenshire coast. Skipper D.F. Noble, 321 Hilton Drive, had been asleep in his cabin when the ship struck, and immediately rushed to the wheelhouse and ordered full astern. The ship was stuck fast, however, and soon water started to flood the engine-room. The siren was blown continuously, rockets were fired, and the crew's bedding was burned to attract attention. Soon the crew could hear rescuers shouting to them from the shore. They were unable to see them in the blinding snow but they were told that the Fraserburgh

lifeboat was on its way. About 2.15 am the *Evergreen* took a heavy list, but an attempt to launch the smallboat was thwarted by heavy seas sweeping over the stern. Skipper Noble ordered his crew to take to the rigging, while the mate and the chief engineer remained in the wheelhouse. The Fraserburgh life-saving apparatus became stuck in the snow on the road between Sandhaven and Rosehearty so a lorry was sent from Rosehearty to meet the rescuers and to bring on the equipment from the stranded trailer. By the time the equipment reached the scene, Fraserburgh lifeboat had arrived and had succeeded in getting close to the *Evergreen* and taking off her nine crewmen, who were brought to Fraserburgh.

5 February 1936   *Pretoria*   A 941   159 Tons/1900

The *Pretoria* was built by Hall Russells for North Shields owners and came to Aberdeen in 1923, owned by A.A. Davidson. While fishing in clear weather six miles SE x S of Buchan Ness lighthouse, at 5 am the *Pretoria* was hauling her gear when she was struck on the port side amidships by the Aberdeen trawler *Georgette* (A 352), and sank in thirty-five minutes.

Skipper William Scarborough, 16 Portland Street, and his eight crewmen were picked up by the *Georgette* and taken to Aberdeen. Skipper Scarborough had been sailing as mate on the *Jane Ross* (A 454) when she was lost at Crail in September 1934.

23 February 1936   *Margaret Stephen*   A 885
213 Tons/1918

Built by Halls, the Strath-class Admiralty trawler *Cornelius Carroll* was sold by the Admiralty in 1922, was registered in the name of Miss Ann G. Lewis and renamed *Boyne Braes* (A 885). Two similar Aberdeen-built Admiralty trawlers were also bought at the same time and registered under the ownership of female members of the Lewis family, being re-named *Bervie Braes* (A 883) and *Doonie Braes* (A 881). *Boyne Braes* passed into the ownership of the Stephen Fishing Co. Ltd.

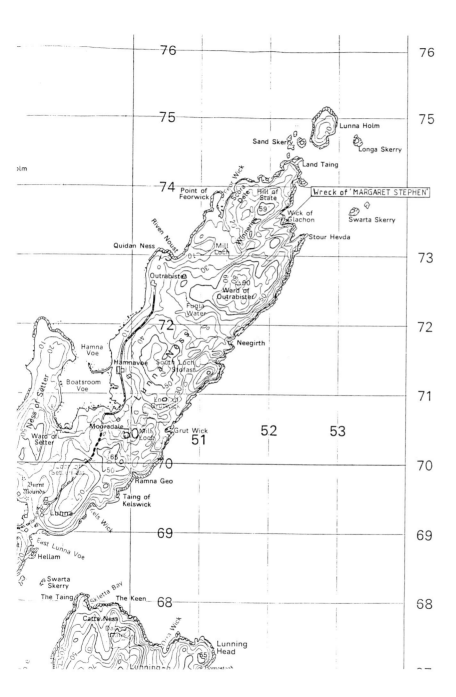

*A map of Lunna Ness, on the east side of the Shetland mainland, showing where the **Margaret Stephen** (A 885) was wrecked in a gale at the Wick of Glachon on 23 February 1936. The area was so sparsely populated that it took the survivors several hours to find the only habitation in the area – a lonely croft at Outrabister, on the opposite side of the peninsula, and not even served by a road at that time. (Courtesy Arthur Robertson, Shetland).*

Aberdeen in October 1932 and was re-named *Margaret Stephen*. At the time of her loss she was on her way to the Flugga fishing grounds to the north of Shetland and was making for the southern entrance to Yell Sound, between the island of Yell and the Shetland mainland. A strong south-easterly gale was blowing and the darkness was so intense that visibility was only about 50 yards. Just before midnight the *Margaret Stephen* struck the rocks near Lunna Ness, on the east side of the Shetland mainland. The ship began to take in water, slowly at first, but soon the crew accommodation was flooded. The ship had no radio to call for assistance, so the crew fired all their distress rockets, as well as some paraffin-soaked netting and all their bedding, and the siren was also sounded until the steam was exhausted. So isolated is the area, however, that none of their signals were seen or heard.

At 3 am, when the ship was being pounded on the rocks by huge seas and the situation was becoming desperate, Skipper Alex Gardner ordered the smallboat to be launched. No sooner had this been done than the *Margaret Stephen* heeled over on to her side, all the lights went out, and the crew had to slide down over the trawler's side to get into their tumbling lifeboat. The trawler slid off the rocks into deeper water, where only the tops of her masts and funnel were visible.

The nine trawlermen now faced a severe struggle to reach the boulder-strewn shore through angry seas, made more dangerous by the backwash from the cliffs surrounding them. Although they were not aware of it at the time, the ship had gone ashore in a tiny inlet in the coastline, with the only beach — albeit a rocky one — on that part of the coast. Despite losing two of their oars, the men succeeded in reaching the beach and scrambling ashore over the boulders. Drenched by seawater and rain, the men did not know where they were and were afraid to separate in case they lost each other. From about 3.30 am until dawn broke some hours later, the men huddled in the scant shelter of an overhanging rock, and then set out in search of a house. After trudging for

several hours over rough moorland in their rubber seaboots, the men eventually spotted the smoke from the only house in the neighbourhood. They were given food and shelter there until news could be sent to Lerwick of the shipwreck and transport was sent for them. Even then, their difficulties were not over — they had to face a further walk of nearly two miles to reach the nearest road.

The ship's bell, inscribed *Cornelius Carroll* 1918, was recovered from among the boulders only in August 1989 by a Shetland amateur diver, Arthur Robertson. After a good clean it was in remarkably good condition after being buffeted in many storms for over half a century.

29 March 1936   *Chancellor*   A 206   156 Tons/1904

The *Chancellor* was built by Hall Russell for Granton owner T.L. Devlin and was brought to Aberdeen in November 1934 by A. King & J.V. Hepburn. Under Skipper W. Knowles, the *Chancellor* was fishing in the Minch twenty miles SW x W from Cape Wrath, when at 3 pm she was seen to be filling with water. As the pumps were unable to cope with the influx, the ship's smallboat was launched. The *Chancellor* sank barely an hour after the leak became apparent, and the crew of nine rowed to the Granton trawler *Zelos* (GN 45), which was fishing nearby. The *Zelos* brought the crew to Granton, as Aberdeen harbour was closed due to rough seas when she arrived off the port.

3 September 1936   *Evelyn*   A 266   235 Tons/1906

Purchased from Hull in 1935 the *Evelyn* had previously fished from Grimsby and Fleetwood, retaining her original name throughout. Under Skipper Robert Robb, 28 Abbey Road, Torry, she was on a fishing trip to the north Iceland grounds and was making for shelter in heavy seas and poor visibility when she ran ashore at Huna Floi, a wide bay on the north coast. The eleven crewmen took to their smallboat and rowed for two hours before landing on a desolate beach. As daylight came they were unable to see any signs of habitation, so took to their boat again and rowed for seven miles until they came across a settlement. It took them a two-day journey to reach Reykjavik, from where they were able to join the mailboat for Leith.

26 October 1936   *Danella*   A 902   197 Tons/1900

The *Danella* was originally the *Braemar* (A 236), a Duthie-built boat which had been sold to Fleetwood in 1908. She was brought back to Aberdeen in 1922 under the ownership of Andrew Lewis and was re-named *Danella* by the Regent Fishing Co. of Aberdeen when they bought her in 1926. While sheltering from a gale, her anchor cable broke and she ran ashore near the Covenanter's Monument at Deerness, on the east of the Orkney mainland. Five of her crew of eight were able to scramble ashore and climb the thirty-foot cliffs to safety. The remaining three, including Skipper David Buchan, climbed ashore later. The *Danella* was successfully pulled from the rocks by a salvage vessel and brought to Aberdeen. She was so badly damaged, however, the repairs would have been uneconomic and she was sold for scrapping.

22 December 1936   *Avondon*   A 136   205 Tons/1905

The *Avondon* had been brought to Aberdeen in 1925 as the *Fishergate* (LO 209), by owner J.A. Harrow, along with her sister *Gillygate* (LO 231), later *Avonglen* (A 137) and lost on 19th September 1934. The *Avondon*, now under the ownership of George R. Wood of Aberdeen was on a trip to Leith for coal when she ran ashore outside Leith harbour at the back of Edinburgh Dock, among a maze of sewer pipes. Her crew got safely ashore but it was found impossible to salvage the *Avondon*, and she soon began to break up, the roof of her wheelhouse, complete with compass and deviation card, being found at Blackness Castle, Bo'ness, several miles further up the Firth of Forth, some weeks later.

19 January 1937   *Golden Sceptre*   A 115   195 Tons/1899

The *Golden Sceptre* had been bought from Hull in 1925 as the *Grecian Empire* (H 479) by John Duffin of Aberdeen, and had sailed from Aberdeen under her original name until she was re-named in May 1934. She sailed from Aberdeen on 19th January 1937 for a fishing trip to Shetland grounds with a crew of nine under Skipper Gordon Grant (43) of 23 Forbes Street, Aberdeen, and was never seen or heard from again. Her smallboat was washed ashore on the island of Fetlar, Shetland. The skipper and the mate, G. Rayworth (44) of 2 Froghall Gardens, Aberdeen, each left a widow and five children.

26 January 1937   *Espera*   A 246   197 Tons/1914

The *Espera* was previously the Hartlepool trawler *Kathleen Burton* (HL 30), built by Hall Russell in 1914 and bought by trawlowner David Wood, Aberdeen in January 1935 and re-named the following month. On her last fishing trip, she suffered severe storm damage and her crew were forced to man the pumps for 36 hours to keep her afloat. She was taken in tow by the German trawler *Este*, of Hamburg, but after the towrope broke twice, the *Este* sent across one of her boats to take off the crew, and the *Espera* finally sank thirty miles SE of Dennis Head, Orkney. The *Este* landed the *Espera's* crew of nine, under Skipper Alex Smith of Ianstown, Buckie, at Buckie.

31 March 1937   *Loch Morar*   A 361   277 Tons/1918

The *Loch Morar* was completed by the Ailsa Shipbuilding Co. Ltd. at Ayr as the Castle-class Admiralty trawler *Giovanni Guinti*. The Admiralty may have regretted allocating such an awkwardly pronounced name, as she was re-named *Idaho* only in 1919. Sold by the Admiralty in 1920, she became the Fleetwood trawler *Cymrea*, before being sold to Hull in 1932, being re-named *Sir Mark Sykes* (H 438). She was bought by the White Star Steam Fishing Co. Ltd. of Aberdeen in October 1935 and re-named *Loch Morar* the following month.

She drove ashore in bad weather on a belt of rocks 1500 yards from the shore at Eyraebakke in south-west

Iceland. Although she carried radio equipment, no signals were heard from her, but a man living nearby had heard the sound of a steam whistle at 3 am, and an hour later saw a rocket fired from out at sea. A motor boat from Eyraebakke set out to render assistance but was unable to get closer to the *Loch Morar* than about 500 yards. There was no sign of life on board, and it was feared that all twelve members of her crew had perished leaving twelve widows and thirty-six children. Her crew, all from Aberdeen, were:-

Skipper: Walter Barber (42)	283 Hilton Drive
Mate: George Duthie (38)	12 Miller Street
Secnd Fisherman: Thomas McKay (29)	45 York Street
Chief Engineer: A. Stevenson	60 Crombie Road
Secnd Engineer: J. Connell	60 Crombie Road
Fireman: C. Milne	60 Crombie Road
Fireman: F. Jackman	76 Victoria Road
Deckhand: John Mitchell (28)	152 Pittodrie Place
Deckhand: John Barrett (52)	89 Virginia Street
Deckhand: W. Brady	15 Balnagask Road
Deckhand: J. Scott	22 St Andrew Street
Cook: D. Lownie	73 Menzies Road

4 November 1937   *Roslin* (2)   A 371   181 Tons/1899

The *Roslin* was a trawler with an unusual history. Built of iron by the firm of D. MacGill of Govan, Glasgow (as the *Windsor Castle* of Hull) she was completed by Cochrane and Cooper of Beverley. Sold foreign she was re-named the *Alcyon*, and then *Wostock*, before becoming the Russian trawler *T6*. She was seized by the Navy in the White Sea on 3rd August 1918, following the Russian revolution, and became the Naval trawler *Greataxe*. Bought from the Navy in July 1920 by John Lewis Ltd. she fished from Aberdeen as the *Greataxe* until being re-named *Roslin* by her new owner, R. Masson, in February 1925.

She sailed from Aberdeen on what was to be her last voyage on 29th October 1937 with a crew of eight. Her usual skipper, Peter Cowie, had smashed a finger with a trawl board two weeks previously and was unable to sail, and the *Roslin* was under the command of the Mate, George Sutherland (35) of 25 College Bounds. About 9.30 on the evening of 4th November the trawler ran ashore just to the south of the mouth of the River Ythan, about a mile from the village of Newburgh, Aberdeenshire. The blasts of her siren were heard by the villagers, and Newburgh lifeboat and the life-saving crews from Collieston and Belhelvie, as well as the Aberdeen lifeboat, were called out. Both lifeboats had actually been called out earlier in the day when the Aberdeen trawler *Delila* (A 182) grounded at Belhelvie and the Newburgh crew had been constantly on duty all day. The Newburgh boat was pulled on its cradle over the sand dunes towards the wreck, but just before they reached the scene all the lights in the ship were extinguished and she could not be seen from the shore.

In the meantime, four of the crew — the two engineers and the two deckhands, George Cowie (20) of 36 Mansefield Place and Kenneth Cormack (57) of 2 Elmfield Place, took to the rigging, while the skipper, second fisherman, cook and fireman sought refuge in the wheelhouse. The ship was being swept continuously by heavy waves along its whole length, and the smallboat and any moveable gear was carried away. The first of the crew to succumb to the constant lashing of the sea was the second engineer (John Jappy (56) 161 West North Street) who lost his hold on the rigging and fell into the sea, being swept away instantly. The three remaining in the rigging could hear their mates in the wheelhouse singing hymns, until another heavy sea carried away the upper wooden half of the wheelhouse and the four men with it.

The watchers on the shore were still unable to pinpoint the position of the wreck in the darkness, so the coastguards stationed their men at intervals along the beach north and south of the approximate position in case of survivors being washed ashore. About 3 am, by which time the remaining three crewmen had been five hours in the rigging, one of the life-saving crew on the

Loch Morar – Two members of the
crew of the **Loch Morar** *(A 361) on
the whaleback while she is berthed
at Point Law, Aberdeen. The man
on the left is Duncan Lownie, who
was cook on the ship when she was
lost with all hands at Iceland on 31
March 1937. The other crew
member has not been identified.
(Photo Courtesy Mrs. A. Watt,
Scalloway).*

Hood – The **Hood** *(A 11) high and
dry on the rocks between Gourdon
and Johnshaven on the
Kincardineshire coast, after running
ashore there on 12 August 1938.
(Photo George Coull Collection).*

beach thought he heard a cry from seaward. The lights of the Aberdeen lifeboat were seen offshore so a message was flashed to it, when just at that moment the *Roslin* was spotted in the lifeboat's search-light beam. Coxswain Tom Sinclair brought his boat as near as possible to the wreck, but was unable to get alongside owing to the heavy waves. As soon as the boat was close enough a line was thrown to the survivors. The rope was caught by Deckhand George Cowie and he was about to secure the rope round the body of Chief Engineer D. Sutherland, when Sutherland lost his grip and fell into the sea, being swept away before anyone could reach him. A second line was thrown and Cowie grabbed this and jumped into the water, to be hauled across to the lifeboat. Deckhand Kenneth Cormack, right at the top of the rigging had another line thrown to him so that he in turn could be pulled over to the lifeboat. The lifeboat finally reached Aberdeen with the two survivors at 5.30 am eight hours after being called out. The six men who were lost were:-

Acting Skipper: George Sutherland (39) 25 College Bounds, wife and four family.

Second Fisherman: Robert Wetherly (39) 41 Ann Street, Widower

Chief Engineer: D. Sutherland (32) 270 Hilton Drive, wife and one young son.

Second Engineer: John J. Jappy (56) 161 West North Street, wife and three family.

Fireman: Charles Grant (32) 6 Commerce Street, Fraserburgh, wife and three young children.

Cook: William Mutch (59) 38 Urquhart Road, widower.

7 May 1938   *Dandini*   A 18   212 Tons/1917

The *Dandini* had been built by Halls for Grimsby owners and came to Aberdeen from Whitby owners in 1924. She was dodging in a strong northerly gale with frequent snow showers off Shetland when at 4 am she collided with the Aberdeen trawler *Barbara Robb* (A 124), which was trawling at the time. The *Dandini* immediately began to fill with water and sank within forty minutes. Skipper James Imlah of Buckie and his eight crewmen

took to their smallboat, from which they were picked up by the *Barbara Robb* and taken to Lerwick.

12 August 1938   *Hood*   A 11   203 Tons/1918

The *Hood* had been built by Hawthorns of Leith as the Strath-class Admiralty trawler *George Hodges*. Sold out of the Navy in 1919, she became the *Hood*, registered in London, and was brought to Aberdeen by Craig Stores in 1934.

Skippered by Alex Slater, 45 Middlefield Place, and carrying a crew of eleven, including an apprentice, she went ashore in dense fog on a ledge of rock opposite Brotherton Castle, between Gourdon and Johnshaven on the Kincardineshire coast, about an hour after high tide. Gourdon lifeboat and the Johnshaven life-saving apparatus were called out. The lifeboat was unable to approach the *Hood*, however, and as the crew appeared to be in no danger, the lifeboat returned to its station after standing by for some time. Efforts to refloat the *Hood* were unsuccessful and she was eventually broken up where she lay.

16 January 1939   *Crisabelle Stephen*   A 374
230 Tons/1906

The *Crisabelle Stephen* had been built by Duthies of Torry for Plymouth owners as the *Albatross* (PH 17). After serving as a minesweeper from 1914 to 1919, she was sold to Fleetwood and from there to Swedish owners in 1924. Re-purchased from Sweden by the Stephen Fishing Co. Ltd. of Aberdeen in 1928, she was re-named *Crisabelle Stephen*.

She sailed from Aberdeen on a fishing trip on a Monday afternoon, and shortly before 6 pm struck the Sea Stone, a large rock on the Scaurs of Cruden, just off the village of Whinnyfold. The Whinnyfold life-saving brigade and Peterhead lifeboat were called out, but, in answer to the *Crisabelle Stephen's* distress rockets the Aberdeen trawler *East Coast* (A 935) and a local fishing yawl stood by. Skipper David Noble of the *East Coast* was a native of Cruden Bay and knew the area intimately, so he was able to bring his ship close to the *Crisabelle Stephen* and pass over a towing hawser. He was successful in refloating the *Crisabelle Stephen* about 7 pm and set off for Aberdeen with the crippled trawler in tow. Meanwhile, the Peterhead lifeboat had arrived on the scene, but as the trawler was now under tow she returned to base. The senior coastguard advised the stations at Collieston and Belhelvie to monitor the progress of the two trawlers as a precautionary measure. At 7.35 pm the Collieston lookout saw the two trawlers passing southwards into patches of mist, but they were never to reach the Belhelvie station. The trawlers had been keeping as close inshore as they dared, and the *East Coast* had been towing for about eighty minutes when, somewhere off the mouth of the River Ythan, the crew of the *East Coast* heard a shout of "Beach her!" and immediately ceased towing. The *Crisabelle Stephen*, which had a slight list to starboard, suddenly rolled over and sank in the misty darkness. One man, Chief Engineer John W. Pirie of 50 Broomhill Road, was spotted in the water, so Fireman F. Wemyss of the *East Coast* jumped into the sea with a rope round his waist and managed to reach the drowning man. The *Crisabelle Stephen's* smallboat drifted near enough for two of the *East Coast's* crew to drop into it and pull to safety the two men in the water. Artifical respiration was applied to Pirie without avail, so after searching the area for some time in the hope of rescuing any further men, the *East Coast* gave up the search and turned for Aberdeen. The names of the nine lost crewmen were:-

Skipper: Francis Fraser (54) c/o 9 Canal Street, widow and one son.
Mate: George McKenzie (38) 107 Walker Road, widow and one son.
Chief Engineer: John W. Pirie, 50 Broomhill Road, widow and one daughter.
Second Engineer: George Proctor (44) 101 Commerce Street, widow.
Second Fisherman: G.W. Fraser (son of the skipper), (32) 37 Market Street, widow and one daughter.
Deckhand: Alex McKenzie (42) 56 Manor Avenue, widow, 2 sons and 5 daughters.
Deckhand: Charles Sivewright (58) c/o 42 Marischal Street, single.
Fireman: John Low (61) 604 Holburn Street, widower with 14 year old daughter.
Cook: James McPherson (43) 73 School Street, Fraserburgh, widow, 3 sons and 2 daughters.

29 June 1939   Stratherrick   A 105   210 Tons/1906

The *Stratherrick*, with her crew of nine under Skipper William Cowie, 16 School Terrace, was fishing fifty miles north-east of the Tyne when she sprang a leak. The North Shields trawler *Agnes H. Hastie* (SN 187), which was fishing nearby, took her in tow and made for North Shields. After six hours towing, however, the leak had worsened considerably and the *Stratherrick* foundered twenty-three miles north-east of the Tyne. The nine crewmen got safely away in their smallboat, from which they were picked up by the *Agnes H. Hastie* and brought to North Shields.

4 October 1939   Stromness   A 380   206 Tons/1907

The *Stromness* was one of Aberdeen's few "hansom cabs" i.e. with the wheelhouse set abaft the funnel at the after end of the engine-room casing, and had originally been the *Mopsa* (H 966). She had been brought to Aberdeen in 1935, and at the time of her loss was returning from a fishing trip when she ran ashore at 9.30 pm on Aberdeen beach, abreast the Beach Ballroom. All shore lights had been extinguished for the blackout, and Skipper Stanley Jones, of Morven Place, said he had been disorientated by the lack of lights. The crew of nine were rescued by breeches buoy from the Bridge of Don rocket brigade. It was found impossible to free the *Stromness* from the sands, and she was broken up where she lay.

15 October 1939   City of York   A 324   202 Tons/1904

The *City of York* had spent most of her life fishing from Fleetwood, and had been brought to Aberdeen only in

1935, retaining her original name. With her crew of nine, under 70 year old Skipper George Marsh, she struck a rock off Tolsta Head, Isle of Lewis. The crew took to their smallboat and rowed around for eleven hours till daylight came and they were able to land near the village of Tolsta. One of the survivors, Ernest Shepherd (64) was to lose his life only five months later when the trawler *Soar* was wrecked near Gourdon.

24 October 1939   *Star of Victory*   A 4   235 Tons/1917

The *Star of Victory*, built by Duthies of Aberdeen as the Admiralty Strath-class trawler *William Ashton*, was re-named temporarily *City of Perth* while on loan to the U.S. Navy from 1919. She reverted to her original name when sold by the Navy and sailed from Grimsby as the *William Ashton* until 1929, when she was bought by the Walker Steam Trawl Fishing Co. Ltd., who re-named her *Star of Victory*. She was wrecked at Keiss, near Wick, but no details of her loss were apparently published under wartime censorship.

20 November 1939   *Delphine*   A 126   250 Tons/1914

The *Delphine* had been fishing from Grimsby under registration GY 958 until brought to Aberdeen by the North Star Steam Fishing Co. Ltd. in 1934. She had been sold to the Boston Deep Sea Fishing & Ice Co. Ltd. of Fleetwood in October 1939, and it is presumed she had a Fleetwood crew when she was sunk by gunfire from the German U-Boat U33 eighteen miles N x E of Tory Island, off Northern Ireland.

5 December 1939   *Quixotic*   A 189   197 Tons/1898

At the time of her loss, the *Quixotic*, 41 years old, was Aberdeen's oldest trawler. Rather similar in appearance to the *Stromness*, lost two months earlier, she had her wheelhouse abaft the funnel, and had fished out of Grimsby as GY 982 until she came to Aberdeen in 1932. With a crew of nine, under Skipper William Gardiner of Cullen, she ran aground in the darkness at the Bell Rock, directly under the lighthouse, which was extinguished at

the time. The lighthouse keepers threw ropes towards the ship but the crew were unable to reach them. The crew then burned their bedding as flares, and these were answered by the Arbroath and Broughty Ferry lifeboats. The Broughty Ferry boat was able to approach closely enough for the crew to jump on board. The crew were:-

Skipper: William Gardiner, 34 Seafield St. Cullen.
Mate: Andrew Innes, Seafield St. Cullen.
Chief Engineer: Oswald McRonald, 25 Laurelwood Avenue, Aberdeen.
Second Engineer: John Pirrie, 8 Victoria Place, Cullen.
Fireman: William Addison, 13 Castle Terrace, Cullen.
Second Fisherman: George Fraser, 215 Hilton Drive, Aberdeen.
Deckhand: George Addison, Seafield St. Cullen.
Deckhand: John Findlay, Earndale, Cullen.
Cook: Alexander Dow, 5 Victoria Place, Cullen.

18 December 1939   *Active* (2)   A 897   185 Tons/1899

The *Active* was the first of a batch of four steam trawlers built by the Irvine Shipbuilding Co. Ltd. for the Peterhead Steam Trawling Co. Ltd., and was allocated the registration number PD 361. All four trawlers were named after Peterhead whalers, the others being *Eclipse* (PD 364), *Hope* (PD 366) and *Rapid* (PD 367). The *Active* was sold in 1922 to Andrew Robertson of Aberdeen and transferred to Aberdeen registration. On the day of her loss she was attacked and sunk by enemy aircraft 48 miles NNW of Rattray Head. One member of the crew, the cook, George Watt, was killed but the other nine members managed to launch the smallboat before the ship sank and were picked up by the Grimsby trawler *Carbineer 11* (GY 1048).

19 December 1939   *Daneden*   A 59   210 Tons/1914

The *Daneden* was built by Hall Russell in 1914 as the Strath Company trawler *Strathebrie*. In 1939 she was sold out of the Strath fleet, being bought by the Regent Fishing Co. Ltd. and re-named *Daneden*. She was bombed and sunk with the loss of all nine of her crew by

City of York – *A photograph of the* **City of York** *(A 324), taken while she was fishing from Fleetwood. She sank after striking a rock off Tolsta Head, Isle of Lewis, on 15 October 1939. (Photo George Coull Collection).*

Lucida – *The* **Lucida**, *later A 175, pictured sailing from Fleetwood in the early 1930's. She was blown up by a mine in the North Sea on 11 January 1940. (Photo George Coull Collection).*

enemy aircraft twelve miles ESE of the island of Fetlar, Shetland.

She had sailed from Aberdeen on 11th December and was fishing not far from the Aberdeen trawlers *Star of Scotland*, which was also attacked and suffered two fatal casualties, and *Strathalbyn*, but, although the other trawlers witnessed the attack on the *Daneden* they were not aware of her identity at that time. Her crew were:-

Skipper: George Bowie, 2 Tullos Circle.
Mate: Thomas Reynolds, 43 Summerfield Terrace.
Chief Engineer: James Morrison, 1 Rosebank Terrace.
Second Engineer: James Broadfoot, 109 Gerrard Street.
Fireman: George Tait, Moray Road, Fraserburgh.
Second Fisherman: James Bowie, 76 Victoria Road.
Deckhand: James Geddes Jnr. 60 Park Street.
Deckhand: William Paterson, 32 Seatown, Buckie.
Cook: William Reid, 21 Bridgend, Buckie.

11 January 1940 *Lucida* A 175 251 Tons/1914

The *Lucida* had been brought to Aberdeen in 1935 by local owners George Robb & Sons Ltd. She was sold to the Boston Deep Sea Fishing Co. Ltd. of Hull in October 1939 but retained her Aberdeen registration. She struck a mine in the North Sea and was lost with all of her crew of twelve, under Skipper A.C. Thundercliffe.

18 March 1940 *Soar* A 284 219 Tons/1915

Like the *Lucida*, the *Soar* had been a Fleetwood trawler until 1935, when she had been bought by Aberdeen owners. She had been on her way back to Aberdeen from a coaling trip with a six-man crew when she ran ashore one mile south of Gourdon on the Kincardineshire coast. The discovery of her loss was made by Mr. W. Mowatt of 20 Caldwell, Gourdon, who was walking along the shore in the early morning when he spotted some wreckage and stumbled over a body. He ran to Gourdon to report the wreck, and the Gourdon lifeboat and life-saving apparatus went to the scene. By this time, however, the trawler was breaking up fast and there was no trace of the crew. During the day five bodies were found among the rocks and taken to Stonehaven for identification. The crew were:-

Skipper: Fred G. Slatter (67), 123 Western Road, Woodside.
Mate: Ernest Sanders (57), 130 Walker Road.
Chief Engineer: Roderick McRae (70), 177 Spital. (A survivor of the *Cassandra* lost on 26th August 1935).
Second Engineer: George Lawrie (57), 24 Ruthrie Road.
Fireman: Ernest Shepherd (64), 9 Castle Street. (A survivor of the *City of York* lost on 15th October 1939).
Cook: Joshua Masson (54), 6 Colville Place.

23 March 1940 *Loch Assater* A 321 210 Tons/1910

The *Loch Assater* had been built by Duthies of Aberdeen for the Empire Steam Fishing Co. Ltd. in 1910 and had retained her original name after being sold to the Stephen Fishing Co. Ltd. in 1925. She had served as a minesweeper in World War 1 and was again taken up for Naval service, this time as an armed patrol trawler, in February 1940. On 23rd March she was severely damaged by a mine in the North Sea and sank shortly afterwards.

Her crew of thirteen got safely away in their smallboat and were picked up after several hours by the Aberdeen trawler *Strathtummel* (A 402).

3 April 1940 *Gorspen* A 376 208 Tons/1913

The *Gorspen* had originally been the North Shields trawler *Loyal Prince* (SN 244), which had been one of the first trawlers to be taken up for minesweeping duties in August 1914, being allocated Pennant No.51. She came to Aberdeen in 1929 under the ownership of C.R. Grimmer, who sold her in 1931 to Messrs. Spence & Gore, who renamed her to incorporate part of each of their names. On the day of her loss she was fishing 31 miles NE of Out Skerries, Shetland when she was bombed and sunk by enemy aircraft.

The crew were picked up from their smallboat by the *Bracondene* (A 615).

Soar – The **Soar**, later A 284, was originally registered in Fleetwood (FD 155) and is pictured leaving there on a fishing trip, probably during the early 1930's. She was wrecked near Gourdon, Kincardineshire on 18 March 1940 with the loss of her coaling crew of six. (Photo George Coull Collection).

Gorspen – The **Loyal Prince** (SN 244) was one of the first trawlers to be taken up by the Navy for minesweeping in World War I. She came to Aberdeen in 1929 and was later re-named **Gorspen** (A 376). She was bombed and sunk by German aircraft off Shetland on 3 April 1940. (Photo George Coull Collection).

69

3 April 1940 *Sansonnet* A 862 212 Tons/1916

The *Sansonnet* was formerly the Grimsby trawler *Lord Stanhope* (GY 285), bought by Aberdeen owners A. Bruce and others in 1922 and re-named in 1926. She was bombed and sunk by enemy aircraft eighteen miles E x S of Muckle Flugga, Shetland with the loss of her crew of ten. The crew were:-

Skipper: W.J. McCallum (53), 7 Menzies Road.
Mate: A.G. McKay (43), 190 Victoria Road.
Chief Engineer: W.N. Lindsay (59), 78 Middlefield Terrace.
Second Engineer: James Murray (38), 5 East Carlton Terrace, Buckie.
Fireman: James Murray (35), 1 John Street, Buckie.
Second Fisherman: J.W. Thompson (37), 118 Victoria Road, (formerly of Hull).
Deckhand: A.C. Hall, 89 Eaton Street, Hull.
Deckhand: William Clark (54), 37 Dee Street.
Deckhand: J.A. McGarry, 126 Campbell Street, Hull.
Cook: David F. Slater (45), 138 Crown Street.

29 April 1940 *Strathalford* A 50 218 Tons/1929

The *Strathalford*, one of the newer trawlers in the well-known Strath fleet, was on her way to the fishing grounds when she ran ashore on rocks in Wick Bay in darkness. When the trawler's plight became known, Wick lifeboat and life-saving apparatus immediately set off for the scene. The crew meanwhile had tried to launch their smallboat, but this was swept away with one of the deckhands, John Findlay, clinging to it. The boat turned upside down but Findlay succeeded in getting astride of the upturned boat, from where he was rescued by Wick lifeboat. The lifeboat was unable to get close to the wreck because of heavy seas, but the life-saving team succeeded in firing a line over the trawler, and the crew, all of whom except the skipper were near the wheelhouse, were able to rig their end of the breeches buoy apparatus and be hauled ashore one by one. Three men were washed away and lost before they could be got ashore, but five men were brought to safety by the life-saving crew. The skipper, John Wood, had taken to the rigging of the foremast and as the trawler's deck was now under water he was unable to reach the breeches buoy attached to the wheelhouse, and had to climb higher out of trhe reach of the waves. Another rocket was fired and the line passed over the *Strathalford's* aerial. The lifeboatmen picked up one end of the line, but it was almost an hour before Skipper Wood managed to secure his end of the line and make his way down the rigging into the sea. He was hauled aboard the lifeboat and he and John Findlay were taken to Wick hospital suffering from exposure.

The three who lost their lives were:-

Chief Engineer: Charles Matheson, 96 Great Northern Road. (10 years service with the Strath Company).
Second Engineer: John B. Sievewright (57), 28 Manor Avenue. (33 years service with the Strath Company).
Cook: Alfred Tytler (64), 3 Coutts Court.

The survivors were:-

Skipper: John Wood (53), 33 Middlefield Place.
Mate: Richard Anderson, 7 Strathlene Road, Findochty.
Second Fisherman: A. Mathieson, 20 Ferrier Crescent.
Deckhand: George Buthlay, 183 Victoria Road.
Deckhand: John Findlay, 216 Seatown, Cullen.
Fireman: A. Adams, 19 Short Loanings.
Fireman: Charles McKay, 90 Gellymill Street, Macduff.

28 May 1940 *Corennie* A 228 203 Tons/1918

The *Corennie* had been built by Scott of Bowling as the Strath-class Admiralty trawler *Robert Gibson*. Sold out of the Navy in 1920, she had retained her original name under both London and North Shields registrations. She was brought to Aberdeen by owners P. & J. Johnstone Ltd. in 1933, and was re-named *Corennie* in August 1934. She is presumed to have been lost in the North Sea by enemy action, with her crew of ten, who were:-

Skipper: G. Burnett.
Mate: George Findlay (27), 101 Victoria Road.
Chief Engineer: Alex S. Adam (57), 47 Menzies Road.

Sansonnet – The **Sansonnet** *(A 862) has just backed out from Aberdeen Fish Market after landing her fish and is turning to look for a berth at Point Law, on the opposite side. She was formerly the **Lord Stanhope** (GY 285), and was bombed and sunk by enemy aircraft on 3 April 1940. (Photo George Coull Collection).*

Elizabeth Angela – The **Hannah E. Reynolds** *(A 322) sailing into Fleetwood Harbour before being re-named **Elizabeth Angela** in 1938. She was taken up for minesweeping in December 1939 and was sunk by enemy bombing near Dover on 13 August 1940. (Photo George Coull Collection).*

Deckhand: William Greig (41), 2 Manor Walk.
Deckhand: James Lindsay (44), 161 Victoria Road.
Cook: Robert C. Buchan (53), 27 Miller Street.
    G. Bruce.
    W.A. Bruce.
    J.W. Christie.
    A.J. Reid.

28 May 1940   *Loch Shin*   A 78   255 Tons/1930

A well-found ship less than ten years old, the *Loch Shin* was taken up by the Admiralty on 28th September 1939, and was converted to become a boom defence vessel. She was bombed and sunk by enemy aircraft at Harstad, Norway.

10 June 1940   *River Ness*   A 940   203 Tons/1918

The *River Ness* was built by Hall Russell as the Admiralty Strath-class trawler *David Buchan*. Her naval career was short, as she was sold in 1919, re-named *River Ness* and registered at Montrose as ME 51. She came to Aberdeen early in 1923 under the ownership of the Misses Hannah and Williamina Lewis, who sold her to Craig Stores in 1932. She was bombed and sunk by enemy aircraft eight miles NE x N of Out Skerries, Shetland, with the loss of eight crewmen. Those who lost their lives were:-

Deckhand: William G. Davidson (17), 48 Mansefield Road.
Engineer: James W. Duncan, 81 Oscar Road. Widow and family of seven.
    E. Garrod.
Cook: Thomas Hartley (58), 12 Ashvale Place. Widow and family of six.
    J.C. Lees.
    G.P. Leslie.
    George Main (25), 24 Gerrard Street.
Second Fisherman: R.V. Wonnacott.

The Skipper, David B. Craig and the mate James Christie were picked up from the sea by the *Bracondene*

(A 615) and taken to Lerwick. The *Bracondene* had picked up the crew of the *Gorspen* (A 376), when she was attacked and sunk by enemy aircraft in the same area on 3rd April.

8 August 1940   *Loch Loyal*   A 733   196 Tons/1907

Built by Halls for Aberdeen's Loch Line Steam Trawl Fishing Co. Ltd, the *Loch Loyal* (A 132) was one of the first Aberdeen trawlers taken up for minesweeping in August 1914. On being released by the Admiralty in 1919 she was sold to Lowestoft owners and bore the registration LT 347. She was bought by Andrew Lewis of Aberdeen in 1922 and registered as A 733, before being sold to George Wood in 1929. She sank in the Moray Firth following a collision with a naval patrol vessel.

13 August 1940   *Elizabeth Angela*   A 322
253 Tons/1928

The *Elizabeth Angela* had been built by Beardsmores of Dalmuir, Glasgow as the *Hannah E. Reynolds* for Aberdeen owners W.A. Leith and Skipper J.F. Reynolds. She was sold in 1937 to the Boston Deep Sea Fishing Co. Ltd. of Fleetwood and re-named in December 1938, but retained her Aberdeen registration. She was taken up for conversion to a minesweeper in November 1939 and sunk by bombing off the Downs near Dover.

23 August 1940   *Flavia*   202 Tons/1919

The *Flavia* had been built at Wivenhoe for the Admiralty as the Strath-class trawler *William Harrison*, but was not required for naval service. She was sold in 1921 and became *Flavia* (GY 1335). She came under the ownership of Joseph Craig of Craig Stores, Aberdeen in 1936. She was lost with her crew of ten in the North Sea, presumably by enemy action.
Her crew were:-

Skipper: R.P. Leiper, 237 Victoria Road.
Mate: George Murray (34), 154 Victoria Road.
Chief Engineer: A.M. Gordon (58), 15 Balmoral Road.

Second Engineer: John Wilson, 21 Castle Street, Keith Inch, Peterhead.
Second Fisherman: Alex Leiper, 39 Mansefield Road.
Deckhand: John Buchan (18), Jamaica Street, Peterhead.
Deckhand: Alfred McIntosh (17), 67 Regent Walk.
Fireman: James Munro (18), 36 Kirkhill Road.
Fireman: James Simpson (28), 28 Marywell Street.
Cook: William Kelly (64), 89 Union Street.

Alex Leiper was a brother of the skipper, and was due to be married on 21st September.

11 September 1940   *Beathwood*   A 442
209 Tons/1912

Built by Halls in 1912 for the Strouds Steam Fishing Co. Ltd. as the *Osborne Stroud*, this trawler had an interesting history. With her sister ship *Daniel Stroud* (A 438) (later *Loch Esk*), the *Osborne Stroud* was purchased by the Admiralty in July 1914 for conversion to a minesweeper and was allocated Pennant No.3. Sold by the Admiralty in 1920, she was bought by J.R. McBeath and others, and re-named *Beathwood*. She was bombed and sunk by enemy aircraft one mile east of Montrose with the loss of six of her crew. Those lost were:-

Skipper: George Wood (48), 146 South Esplanade West.
Chief Engineer: James N. Ruddiman, 15 Hilton Street. (A crewman on the *Dorothy Gray* when she rammed and sank U18 in Scapa Flow in 1914).
Second Engineer: John Milne, 15 Nelson Street.
Deckhand: A.G. Mair, 62 Prospect Terrace.
  W. Findlay.
  W.G. Findlay.

The *Beathwood* had rescued the crew of the *Avonglen*, which was lost in September 1934.

24 September 1940   *Bass Rock*   A 759   169 Tons/1907

The *Bass Rock* was built in Leith for the Leith Steam Fishing Co. Ltd. and registered as LH 296. She served as a minesweeper (Pennant 513) from September 1914 to 1919, before being sold to Lowestoft owners and reg-

istered as LT 646, keeping her original name. She was brought to Aberdeen in 1922 by Thomas Stephen and fished from the port until 1930 when she was sold to Milford Haven owners W.H. East, but she continued to be registered in Aberdeen. She was bombed and sunk by enemy aircraft off the Old Head of Kinsale, Ireland, with the loss of Skipper A. Skewis and three crew members.

11 January 1941   *Oriole*   A 305   172 Tons/1907

The *Oriole* was originally one of the large fleet belonging to Kelsall Brothers & Beeching Ltd. of Hull, all named after birds, and was registered as H 926. She was taken up by the Admiralty in October 1914 and served as a minesweeper (Pennant 636) till 1919. She was bought by Skipper William McPherson in 1935 and used as a steam line fishing vessel. She struck a mine 2 miles north of Stakken North Point, Faroe, and was lost with her whole crew of ten, who were:-

Skipper: William McPherson (50), 204 Victoria Road. Left nine daughters.
Chief Engineer: James Wood (41), 72 Victoria Road. Widow and four family.
Second Engineer: W.J.G. Bruce (26), 60 Wellington Street. Widow and one child.
William G. Bruce DSM (56), 63 Wales Street. (Father of above).
J.I. Hosie, 29 Elmbank Terrace.
F.A. King.
Harold Osborne (42), 16 Balnagask Road (formerly of Hull).
W. Reid (64), 3 Menzies Road.
W. Todd.
W. Wood, 26 Ferry Road.

12 January 1941   *Strathyre*   A 597   212 Tons/1916

The *Strathyre*, and her sister *Strathlochy* (A 596) were taken up immediately after completion by Hall Russell for service as minesweepers and served till 1919. Altogether no less than 41 Strath trawlers were in the Navy in World War 1. The *Strathyre* was sunk by a magnetic mine off Great Orme Head while fishing from

Fleetwood. There is no record of any casualties.

23 January 1941   *Arora*   A 320   192 Tons/1903

The *Arora* had been built as the *Rubislaw* (A 907) for the Rubislaw Steam Fishing Co. Ltd. of Aberdeen. In 1912 she was sold to Norway and re-named *Hodd* and later *Brim*, before being brought back to Aberdeen under the latter name by Adam Brothers Ltd. in 1920. She was sold to A. Robertson of Aberdeen in 1922 and re-named *Arora*. She took a prominent part in the efforts to rescue the crew of the *Ben Doran* in 1930, bringing the life-saving apparatus to the scene. The *Arora* had also rescued the crew of the *Florence Dombey* when she sank on 5th May 1933. She was lost in the North Sea, apparently by enemy action, with her crew of nine, who were:-

Skipper: G.W. Smith.
Mate: A.D. Craig, 4 Tullos Circle. (Acting skipper in a previous attack on the ship).
   Robert Craig (22), 38 Charlotte Street.
   A. Falconer.
   G. Findlay.
   William McLean (63), 62 Castlehill Barracks.
   George Robertson (21), 178 Victoria Road.
   George Sinclair (51), 24 Garthdee Crescent.
   Alex Sutherland (37), 39 Menzies Road.

26 February 1941   *Christabelle*   A 360   203 Tons/1917

The *Christabelle* was built by Hall Russell as the Strath-class Admiralty trawler *John Barry* and served as a minesweeper till being sold in 1921, when she was re-named *Christabelle* under Grimsby owners. She was bought by J.J. MacRae of Aberdeen in 1928. Like the *Oriole* in January she struck a mine in Faroese waters, off Fuglo Head, and was lost with her crew of ten:-

Skipper: John C. Craig (49), Hazelbank, Nigg.
   Harry Goodwin (26), 30 James Street.
   George Harper (48), 19 Littlejohn Street.
   Harry Lead, c/o 132 Glenbervie Road.
   James C. McBain (40), 25 Manor Avenue.

   Alex S.O. Niven (46), 24 Hill Street.
   Joseph Rasmussen (67), 23 Wallfield Crescent.
   Peter Riley (49), 3 Ferrier Crescent.
   J.C. Sutherland.
   Sidney S. Weir (24), 51 Marischal Street.

Crewmen James McBain and Alex Niven had both been in the Army in World War 1, as had Chief Engineer Peter Riley, who left a widow and ten of a family.

27 March 1941   *Kinclaven*   A 17   178 Tons/1924

The *Kinclaven* was built by Duthies for the Leipers, the well-known line-fishing family of Aberdeen, and used by them as a steam liner. She is presumed to have been lost through enemy air attack off Faroe, with her crew of ten.

Skipper: William Main (44), 219 Victoria Road.
   James Christie.
   John Christie (45), 23 Brimmond Place.
   J. Gardiner.
   John Gault (47), 7 Grampian Road.
   William Main (40), 13 Commerce Street.
   Edward Moore, 19 Bedford Avenue.
   John Phillips (62), 46 Grampian Circle.
   John L. Wood (53), 190 Victoria Road.
   Thomas B. Wood, 56 Manor Avenue, (who had served in the Royal Navy in World War 1 and again for a time in World War II).

29 March 1941   *Horace E. Nutten*   A552   209 Tons/1913

The *Horace E. Nutten* had been built for the Aberdeen Steam Trawl Fishing Co. Ltd. as the *Strathcarron*, and under that name had been one of the first trawlers to be taken up for the Navy in August 1914, being allocated Pennant No.98. She came back to Aberdeen in 1919 and fished for her original owners till being sold in 1929 to Albert and Horace Nutten and re-named *Horace E. Nutten*. It is interesting that Skipper Horace Nutten was her first skipper in 1913. She was bombed and sunk by enemy aircraft in the Moray Firth, with the loss of her crew of ten:-

Skipper: Tom E. Nutten (56), 37 Grampian Road. Widow and eight family.

Mate: Alex Flockhart, 47 Glenbervie Road. Widow and two family.

Alex Allen (60), 35 Park Road. Widow and seven family.

George Anderson (41), 32 Seaton Place East. Widow and three family.

Henry Charlton (61), 188 Victoria Road. Widow and eight family.

John Connor (29), 22 St. Andrew Street. Widow and three daughters.

Keith M. Cowie (52), 69 Shiprow.

Joseph Dawson, 21 Seaton Road. Widow and eight family.

Peter Edwards (45), 16 Tullos Place. Widow and four family. (A survivor of the *Margaret Clark*, lost on 10th December 1933).

Fred G. Foster (33), 19 Glenbervie Road. (Single — nephew of skipper)

John Connor, a fireman, had only been nine months at sea. Previously he had been a French polisher and had worked on the *Queen Mary* when she was being built. He was a keen ballroom dancer, well known in Aberdeen ballrooms.

30 March 1941   *Nisus*   A 318   210 Tons/1917

The *Nisus* was the former Strath-class Admiralty trawler *James Archibald*, built by Duthies of Aberdeen. Sold in 1921, she was registered in London LO 418 until being bought by David Wood of Aberdeen in 1928 and re-named *Nisus*. She was operated as a steam line fishing vessel and was presumed lost by enemy action in Faroese waters. Her crewmen were:-

Skipper: George Christie (52), 192 Victoria Road.

William I.M. Robb (44), 34 Abbey Road.

William R. Wood (47), 236 Victoria Road.

William Craig (45), 33 Walker Road.

A. Findlay DCM, MM.

J.W. Findlay.

David Gault (42), 2 Ferrier Gardens.

George Holmes (48), 58 Abbey Road.

John Main (37), 7 Abbey Place.

James Tyson (39), 125 Sinclair Road.

(James Tyson had been discharged from the Army on health grounds after being evacuated from Dunkirk.)

7 April 1941   *Rochebonne*   A 433   258 Tons/1913

Along with her sister *Chassiron* (later A 435) the *Rochebonne* was purchased from La Rochelle, France, by J. Mackie & A. Robertson Jnr. in December 1936. She was taken up by the Navy for minesweeping in February 1940 and was bombed and sunk in the English Channel.

4 May 1941   *Ben Gairn*   A 738   234 Tons/1916

Completed by Hall Russell in November 1916 for Richard Irvin & Sons Ltd. the *Ben Gairn* was immediately taken up by the Navy and served in minesweeping and patrol duties till 1919. She was again taken up by the Navy in June 1940 as a minesweeper and was sunk by a parachute mine off Lowestoft.

1 July 1941   *Strathgairn*   A 251   211 Tons/1915

The *Strathgairn* was completed by Hall Russell for the Aberdeen Steam Trawling & Fishing Co. Ltd. in March 1915 and was immediately taken up by the Navy as a minesweeper, serving in this capacity till 1919. She was lost by a mine explosion twenty miles south-west of Barra Head, Outer Hebrides. Five of her crew were lost:-

H. Ashton.
H.J. Brown.
E.W. Curtis.
F.C. Dawkins.
T. Reid.

11 July 1941   *Suzette*   A 346   199 Tons/1920

Completed by Ritchie, Graham & Milne of Whiteinch, Glasgow for the Admiralty as a Strath-class trawler, the *Edward Grey* was too late for naval service and in 1921 she was sold to Grimsby owners, re-named *Suzette* and registered as GY 1330. She was bought by the Gorspen Steam Trawling Co. Ltd. of Aberdeen in 1935 and registered as A 346, changing owners again in 1937 to

Kinclaven – The steam line-fishing vessel **Kinclaven** (A 17) being launched from Duthie's Yard, Torry, in 1924. She was presumed lost by enemy air attack off Faroe on 27 March 1941 with her crew of ten. (Photo Aberdeen Museum).

Ocean Victor – The foredeck of the **Ocean Victor** (A 7) as seen from the bow. She was lost, presumably by enemy action, in August 1941 with her crew of 13 on a fishing trip to Iceland. (Photo Courtesy David B. Craig).

A.A. Davidson and in 1940 to Malcolm Smith Ltd. She is recorded as having stranded on the Girdle Reef, Peterhead, but no further details have been published.

27 July 1941 *Ben Strome* A 109 198 Tons/1914

Built with her sister *Ben Barvas* by Hall Russell in 1914 for Richard Irvin & Sons Ltd. the *Ben Strome* remained under their ownership for the whole of her lifetime. She was taken up by the Navy as a minesweeper in April 1915 and was retained in that capacity until 1919, when she was released to commence her fishing career. The *Ben Strome* was attacked and sunk by German aircraft fifteen miles south-west of Fuglo Island, Faroe, with the loss of her crew of ten:-

Skipper: Fred Baker, 28 Grampian Road.
Mate: John Fyfe (51), 16 Cotton Street. Widow and five family. (Survivor of the *Margaret Clark* lost on 10th December 1933).
Deckhand: George Hay (55), 39 Albion Street. Widow and five family.
Fireman: John Reith (33), 57 Castlehill Barracks. Widow and one daughter.
Fireman: Andrew Smith (20), 5 Ferrier Gardens.
Cook: Alex Duncan, 39 Grampian Place.
Alex Aspinall, 387 Nth Anderson Drive. (Awarded the DSM in World War 1).
Albert Deans (39), 70 Nelson Street. Widow and one son.
John Edmond (52), 165 School Drive. Widow and three family.
Edward Studd (38), 15 Balnagask Road. Widow and five family.

28 July 1941 *Strathlochy* A 596 212 Tons/1916

The *Strathlochy* and her sister the *Strathyre* (A 597) were a pair of trawlers completed for owner John Brown's Aberdeen Steam Trawling & Fishing Co. Ltd. in January 1916. Both ships were immediately taken up for minesweeping until 1919 and by a strange coincidence both were lost by enemy action in 1941. The *Strathlochy*

was bombed and sunk by enemy aircraft 180 miles NW of Rora Head, Orkney. There is no record of casualties.

The *Strathlochy* was the prototype vessel for the 149 Admiralty trawlers of the Strath-class, her builders plans being taken as the standard for the class.

5 August 1941 *Ocean Victor* A 7 202 Tons/1918

The *Ocean Victor* had been built as the Admiralty Strath-class *John Fairman* by Rennie Forrestt of Wivenhoe, Essex. Sold by the Admiralty in 1920, she was re-named *Ocean Victor* and was registered first in London, then in Hull and later in Grimsby before being bought by George Craig and others of Aberdeen in February 1929 and given the registration A 7. She called at Reykjavik on 5th August 1941 while on a fishing trip to Iceland waters and was never seen again. She is presumed to have been lost by enemy action. Her crew were:-

Skipper: Marquis Slater (43), 14 Beechgrove Avenue. Widow and 5 daughters.
Mate: Ben Nicholson (44), 3 Balnagask Road. Widow and seven family. (Survivor of the *Emperor* lost 10th February 1926).
Sec. Fisherman: James Slater (38), 66 Victoria Road. Widow and two children.
Chief Engineer: James Bolton (46), 12 Rosebank Place.
Second Engineer: Alex S. Innes (49), 6 Blacks Buildings.
Deckhand: Alex Innes (32), 6 Ferrier Crescent.
Deckhand: Kenneth McKay (44), 42 Marischal Street.
Cook: George Goodbrand (43), 7 Ferrier Crescent.
Alex Addison (25), 88 Summer Street.
Herbert Burnett (15) 11 Ferrier Crescent.
James Main (40) 30 Jute Street.
J. Hejnesen   D. Joensen.
Herbert Burnett, a lad of fiteen, was on his first trip. His father was dead, and his mother had a family of seven to bring up.

6 September 1941 *Strathborve* A 139 216 Tons/1930

The *Strathborve*, with her sister *Strathblair* (A 132), were among the few Aberdeen trawlers which were under ten years old at the outbreak of World War II. She was taken up for Naval service in August 1940 and was mined and sunk in the Humber area.

30 September 1941 *Star of Deveron* **A 55**
220 Tons/1915

The *Star of Deveron* had experienced several changes of name, registration port, owners, even nationality, in her twenty-six years. Completed by Hall Russell in October 1915 for the Walker Steam Trawl Fishing Co. Ltd. as the *Star of Peace* (A 481), she was taken up as a minesweeper in November 1915 and was a naval vessel until 1919. She was sold to Belgium in 1922, being re-named *Noordzee 11*, before being sold to Granton owner A.G. Brown, who re-named her *Merleton* (GN 97). In 1934 she was bought by Wilson Buchan of Victoria Road, who re-named her *Mary Buchan* (A 55). In 1938 she was again sold, being bought this time by Thomas Walker of Aberdeen, who re-named her *Star of Deveron*. She was taken up for patrol and minesweeping duties in November 1939 and was destroyed by bombing at North Shields.

30 September 1941 *Eileen Duncan* **A 413**
223 Tons/1910

Built by Cochranes of Selby for Liverpool owners and registered LL 36, the *Eileen Duncan* had seen naval service from 1915 to 1919. She was sold to Aberdeen owners W. & G.R. Wood in July 1936 and registered in Aberdeen, retaining her original name. She was again taken up for minesweeping in January 1940, and was destroyed by German bombs at North Shields.

16 November 1941 *Fernbank* **A 910** **211 Tons/1907**

The *Fernbank* had been built by Hall Russell for the White Star Steam Fishing Co. Ltd. as the *Loch Kildonan* (A 163). She was taken up by the Navy at the outbreak of war and allocated Pennant No. 107 as a minesweeper. She was sold to the Montrose Fishing Co. Ltd. in 1919 and re-named *River Annan* (ME 249), but her career in

Montrose was short and she returned to Aberdeen in August 1922 as the *Fernbank* under the ownership of Thomas Stephen, and later the Stephen Fishing Co. Ltd. She was bombed and sunk by enemy aircraft twelve miles north-west of Mygganaes Light, Faroe, with the loss of four of her crew:-

Cook: James Percy (51), 137 Glenbervie Road.
Fireman: James Petrie (43), 9 Girdlestone Place.
  David Runcie (64), 128 Walker Road.
  William Stevenson (61), 88 Constitution Street.

James Petrie had served in the Black Watch in World War 1 and had spent some time as a prisoner of war.

10 December 1941 *Kincorth* **A 263** **148 Tons/1909**

The *Kincorth* was built by Duthies for the well-known Leiper family of line fishers, and was owned by them till 1926, when she was sold to G. Gray and others, who sold her in 1930 to Richard Irvin & Sons Ltd. She retained her original name throughout her life, and in her later years was based in Fleetwood, with a Fleetwood crew. She was sunk by a mine explosion seven miles ENE of Lynas Point, North Wales, with the loss of her crew of eleven, under Skipper W.C. Bowles of Fleetwood.

20 January 1942 *Elswick* **A 97** **215 Tons/1906**

Built by Scott & Sons of Bowling for Fleetwood owners, the *Elswick* served as a minesweeper in the Royal Navy from 1915 to 1919, before being sold to Grimsby owners. She was brought to Aberdeen in 1925 under the ownership of T.T. Irvin, and ownership was transferred to Mrs. Ethel Irvin in 1931. She became a total loss after running ashore near Peterhead and was subsequently broken up.

29 January 1942 *Braconbush* **A 770** **204 Tons/1920**

The *Braconbush* was built by Hawthorns of Leith as the Strath-class Admiralty trawler *John Conne*, but was too late to be used for naval service. She was bought by the Don Fishing Co. Ltd. in November 1921 and re-named

Kincorth – The **Kincorth** (A 263) was built as a steam line-fishing vessel and was therefore not fitted with a winch or trawl gallows. She was mined while fishing from Fleetwood on 10 December 1941 with the loss of her crew of eleven. This photograph was obviously taken on her trial trip, when the female passengers seem to have outnumbered the males. Note the compass adjuster on the wheelhouse roof. (Photo Aberdeen Museum).

Braconbush the following month. She was sold to the Boston Deep Sea Fishing & Ice Co. Ltd. of Fleetwood in April 1941, along with her "sister" *Braconburn* (A 768). She was sunk by a mine explosion off Duncansby Head, apparently without loss of life.

15 March 1942 *Danearn* A 395 231 Tons/1916

The *Danearn* had been built by Duthies for the East Coast Steam Fishing Co. Ltd. as the *Pelagos* (A 623), and was a Royal Navy minesweeper till 1919. In 1922 she was sold to William Carnie of Granton and registered as GN 93. She was bought by the Regent Fishing Co. Ltd. (Aberdeen) in January 1936 and re-named *Danearn* (A 395). She ran ashore near Scotstoun Head, north of Peterhead and became a total loss.

12 May 1942 *Ben Ardna* (2) A 417 226 Tons/1917

The *Ben Ardna* was completed by Hall Russell as the Strath-class Admiralty trawler *John Bradford*, and launched on the same day as the *William Barlow*, later to be the Aberdeen trawler *Dorileen* (A 412). She was bought from the Admiralty in 1920 by Richard Irvin & Sons Ltd. along with the *William Barlow* and re-named *Ben Ardna*. She was again taken up by the Navy on 26th August 1939 and employed as an examination vessel in the Tyne area. She was lost in collision whilst in that capacity.

The first *Ben Ardna* (A 517) had been lost while on naval service in 1915.

15 December 1942 *Loch Wasdale* A 457 210 Tons/1915

The *Loch Wasdale* was built by Duthies for the White Star Steam Fishing Co. Ltd. but was immediately taken up by the Royal Navy, serving as a minesweeper till 1919. Ownership was transferred to Malcolm Smith Ltd. of Aberdeen in 1939. She was stranded on the Skerry Rock, off Boddam, in a gale. Captain James Winter (69), the harbour master at Peterhead, took charge of Peterhead lifeboat in the absence through illness of her regular coxswain. He succeeded in manoeuvering the lifeboat alongside the wreck, despite twelve-foot waves, so that each of the twelve-man crew was able to jump aboard the lifeboat. Shortly after the crew were taken off, the *Loch Wasdale* took fire, and she and her large catch of fish had disappeared within three hours.

25 December 1942 *Star of Learney* A 387 207 Tons/1918

The *Star of Learney* was another trawler with an interesting and chequered history. Completed for the Admiralty by Rennie Forrestt of Wivenhoe as the Strath-class trawler *George Ireland*, she was re-named *Teviot* by the Navy in 1920 and retained till 1923, when she was sold to Boston owners and re-named *Firsby*. She was later transferred to Grimsby registration, and in 1929 was sold to Granton owners as the *Rosebery* (GN 104). She was sold in 1936 to the Walker Steam Trawl Fishing Co. Ltd. who re-named her *Star of Learney* (A 387). She was stranded near Kirkwall on Christmas Day 1942, and as she was declared a constructive total loss, her fishing registration was cancelled in April 1943. However, the ship was refloated, repaired and made seaworthy, so she was registered again in October 1943, this time as A 564. She was re-named *River Learney* in 1947, and sailed from Aberdeen under that name until she finally went to the breakers in 1960.

27 March 1943 *Lord Wimborne* A 441 215 Tons/1911

Built by Smiths Dock, Middlesbrough, for Blyth owners, the *Lord Wimborne* was transferred to Grimsby registration GY 916 in 1913. Apart from service as a minesweeper from November 1914 to 1919, the *Lord Wimborne* continued to fish from Grimsby until she was bought by J.S. Kelman of Aberdeen in March 1937, when she took Aberdeen registration but retained her original name. After several changes of owner, she was bought by the Boston Deep Sea Fishing & Ice Co. Ltd. of Fleetwood in January 1941. She ran ashore at Alftanes, Iceland and became a total loss.

25 October 1943 *William Stephen* **A 24**
235 Tons/1917

Built by Duthies of Aberdeen as the Strath-class Admiralty trawler *Joseph Annison*, and retaining her original name after sale by the Admiralty in 1922, the *Joseph Annison* was bought from Grimsby by the Stephen Fishing Co. Ltd. in 1929 and re-named *William Stephen*. She was taken over by the Navy in November 1939 for patrol duties as one of the almost one hundred trawlers pressed into service at the height of the magnetic mine menace. Most of the hundred ships were retained for only a matter of weeks until a mine was recovered and the antidote in the shape of an electric sweep was devised, but the *William Stephen* was transferred to minesweeping duties. She was torpedoed and sunk by a German E-Boat off Cromer, Norfolk.

25 January 1944 *Misten Braes* **A 362** **193 Tons/1915**

The *Misten Braes* was built by Hall Russell in 1915 as the *Marguerite*, and was bought by Granton owner William Carnie and re-named *Zelos* (GN 75). She was sold to A. Robertson of Aberdeen in 1928 and re-named *Arosa* (A 362). The choice of name was somewhat odd as the same owner already had the *Aro* and the *Arora*, and this must have given rise to confusion on the part of suppliers of stores to the various ships. Be that as it may, the *Aro* was sold to North Shields in 1930, and in 1935 the *Arosa* was re-named the *Misten Braes*. She continued fishing during the war and ran ashore at Funnding Fjord, Faroe, becoming a total loss.

30 July 1944 *Braconburn* **A 768** **203 Tons/1918**

The *Braconburn* was originally the Strath-class Admiralty trawler *Richard Briscoll*, completed by Hall Russell in October 1918. Sold by the Navy in 1921, she was bought by the Don Fishing Co. Ltd, along with three other ex-Admiralty trawlers which were also given "Bracon" names, and re-named *Braconburn*. Along with the *Braconbush*, the *Braconburn* was sold to the Boston Deep Sea Fishing & Ice Co. Ltd. of Fleetwood in April

1941. In 1944 she was requisitioned by the Admiralty for use as a blockship, and was on passage to Scapa Flow when she was sunk in collision near the Bell Rock with the American liberty ship *Le Baron Russell Briggs*, with the loss of six of her crew.

17 September 1944 *Mirabelle* **A 176** **203 Tons/1918**

The *Mirabelle* was yet another ex-Admiralty trawler, having been launched by Hall Russell in November 1918 as the Strath-class *Edward Barker*. She was sold in 1921 to Grimsby owners, who re-named her *Mirabelle* (GY 1336). She was bought by the Gorspen Steam Trawling Co. Ltd. of Aberdeen in 1934, and sold on to A.A. Davidson of Aberdeen in 1937. She was requisitioned by the Navy in November 1939, and used first for patrol duties, and later as a fuel carrier. She was a constructive total loss after being severely damaged in a collision.

20 April 1945 *Ethel Crawford* **A 36** **200 Tons/1919**

The last Aberdeen trawler to be lost in World War II, the *Ethel Crawford* had been built by Scotts of Bowling as the Strath-class Admiralty trawler *John Langshaw*. She was completed too late for naval service, and was sold in 1919 to Fleetwood owners, who re-named her *Ethel Crawford*. She was bought by Aberdeen trawlowner Richard Lewis in 1924, and came under the ownership of North-Eastern Fisheries Ltd. in 1932. In 1941 she was sold to the Ardrossan Trawling Co. Ltd. and at the time of her loss was trawling in the Firth of Clyde when she was blown up by a magnetic mine laid by U218 two days previously. There were no survivors from her crew of ten:-

Skipper: A.M. Scales.	T. Shanley.
W. Bowman.	A.S. Shields.
T. Drysdale.	R.H.C. Wright.
R. Ewing.	
J.W. Geddes.	
J.J. Henry.	
T.T. Ritchie.	

Corena – Pictured here in Aberdeen Harbour in the blue and silver funnel colours of Craig Fishing (Aberdeen) Ltd., the **Corena** (A 198) was purchased from the Admiralty on her release from minesweeping service in 1946. She was considerably larger than the average Aberdeen trawler of the time, and was lost at Greenland in September 1948. (Photo George Coull Collection).

Strathelliot – The **Strathelliot** (A 46) high and dry in Hoy Sound, Orkney after running ashore in a severe gale on 23 October 1952. Her crew of 12 were rescued by Stromness Lifeboat. (Photo George Coull Collection).

21 December 1945 *Leith NB* **A 389   203 Tons/1914**

The suffix "NB" applied to ships owned by Granton trawlowners Dow & Carnie was presumably the abbreviation for "North Britain", a name now seldom heard but which was in vogue at the time when the ships, all named after districts in Edinburgh, e.g. *Trinity NB*, *Newhaven NB* etc. were built. The *Leith NB* was built by Hall Russell for Dow & Carnie and was registered GN 22. After naval service till 1919, she was sold to Fleetwood owners, but was brought back to Granton by T.L. Devlin Ltd. and registered as GN 26. She came to Aberdeen in 1936, owned by A. King, was registered as A 389 and retained her original name. At the time of her loss the *Leith NB* was fishing in calm weather twenty-seven miles west by north of Noup Head, Westray, Orkney and was hauling in her trawl when one of the trawl doors came into violent contact with the trawler's hull and punched a hole in the ship's side. The *Leith NB*'s wireless had broken down, so Skipper Alexander King resorted to sounding the siren in the hope that some other trawler might be fishing near enough to hear it. After some time, when there was no sign of help arriving, the crew took to their smallboat, and shortly afterwards the North Shields trawler *Ben Glas* (SN 336) came on the scene, the crew having heard the *Leith NB*'s siren while on passage to Faroe. The *Leith NB* sank shortly after her crew had been rescued, and the *Ben Glas* turned about to land the rescued crew in Kirkwall, along with their smallboat. Those rescued were:-

Skipper: Alexander King.
Mate: Joseph Greig.
Chief Engineer: George Noble.
Second Engineer: A. Raeburn.
R. Sim.   G. Murdoch.   J. Murray.   G. Ross.
Jas. Crockwell.   W. Twidale.   R. Stockless.

3 March 1946 *Star of the East* (2) **A 434**

218 Tons/1912

Built by Hall Russells for the Walker Steam Trawl Fishing Co. Ltd. the *Star of the East* was one of the first Aberdeen trawlers to be taken up for minesweeping at the outbreak of war in 1914. She returned to fishing in 1919 and in 1920, with her sister the *Star of the Isles*, she was sold to the Co-Operative Fishing Society in Scarborough and registered SH 321. In 1941 she returned to Aberdeen, having been purchased by her original owners, the Walker Steam Trawl Fishing Co. Ltd. At the time of her loss, she was on a fishing trip to Iceland and ran aground on Heimaey Island, one of the Westmann Islands, becoming a total loss. Her crew of thirteen were rescued.

? September 1948 *Corena* **A 198   352 Tons/1924**

Built as the *Andalusite* at Beverley for the Kingston Steam Trawling Co. Ltd. of Hull, the *Corena* passed into the ownership of Marrs of Fleetwood in 1933. She was purchased by the Admiralty in the summer of 1939 for conversion to minesweeping, and she spent her next seven years in that capacity, until being sold in 1946 to Joseph Craig, of Aberdeen. She was on a voyage to Greenland waters with a crew of fourteen, all but five of whom were from Hull and Grimsby, and was passing through "a mass of icebergs" when she suddenly ran aground. She listed badly to port and when the plates could be heard crunching on the rocks, the crew launched their lifeboat and got into it. Several hours later a rescue party of Eskimos arrived in a motorboat and took them in tow to the small village of Frederikshavn. From there they were taken in a Danish gunboat 110 miles to Feringhavn, a trading station used by the Faroese fishing smacks for storing salt fish before sailing home with their whole catch. There they remained for nine days before passages could be obtained on Faroese smacks to Torshavn, from where they were able to take passage home on other ships.

26 January 1950 *Kuvera* **A 384   202 Tons/1919**

The *Kuvera* was originally the Strath-class Admiralty trawler *John Heath*, completed by the Ouse Shipbuilding Co. of Hook, Goole in June 1919, too late to be of use in her intended role as a naval vessel. She was bought by Consolidated Fisheries Ltd. of Grimsby, registered GY 381

~and was sold to Aberdeen owners R. Baxter and others in 1936. She was taken over by the Admiralty in July 1940 and served for the remainder of the war as an armed patrol vessel. By the time she was released in September 1945 she had been sold to Granton owners and was carrying a Granton crew when she was lost. She sprang a leak and foundered while fishing 110 miles NE of Buchan Ness in company with the *Chiltern* (GN 25). Her crew of thirteen were rescued by the *Chiltern* under Skipper John Paterson of Newhaven, and brought to Granton.

5 October 1952 *Braconlea* A 227 200 Tons/1920

The *Braconlea* was built by Alexander Hall & Sons for Yarmouth owners as *Donum Maris* (YH 227), but was sold to the Don Fishing Co. Ltd. on completion and registered as A 227 by a special allocation from the Registrar General of Shipping. She was re-named *Braconlea* in July 1921.

She was sold in 1941 to the Boston Deep Sea Fishing & Ice Co. Ltd. of Fleetwood, but retained her name and number and in 1946 was bought by John W. Johnstone of Aberdeen. At the time of her loss she was making for shelter from a gale in Mid Yell Voe, Shetland when she crashed on submerged rocks at the Baas of Hascosay, at the entrance to the Voe. The *Braconlea* immediately began to fill with water so the crew launched the smallboat and summoned assistance by radio and siren. The Aberdeen based trawler *George H. Hastie* (SN 274) was already sheltering in the Voe and made for the *Braconlea* with a local boat, manned by residents, in tow. The *Braconlea*'s boat, with two men, was towed to the *George H. Hastie* by a local motorboat, and the remaining ten crewmen, including Skipper William Summers, were taken off by local boats and taken to the *George H. Hastie*. The crew were landed at Mid Yell, where they stayed overnight until, with the exception of the Skipper and Chief Engineer, they were brought home to Aberdeen by the *Strathleven* (A 47), belonging to the same owner.

23 October 1952 *Loch Lomond* A 299
310 Tons/1930

The *Loch Lomond* was built by Smiths Dock of Middlesbrough for Fleetwood owners as the *Lune* (FD 59). Taken up for minesweeping on 2nd September 1939, she was later converted to become a wreck dispersal vessel until being released by the Navy in June 1946. After a spell in Grimsby registration as GY 538 under the ownership of Malcolm Smith Ltd, she was transferred to Aberdeen in April 1947, and was re-named *Loch Lomond* in March 1948. On the day of her loss the *Loch Lomond* was leaving Aberdeen on a trip to Faroe waters in the company of the *Loch Laggan* (A 82). Heavy seas were running in the harbour entrance channel and the *Loch Laggan* received a severe buffeting on her way to the open sea. The *Loch Lomond*, following some distance astern of her, met some heavy seas and appeared to strike her rudder on the bottom halfway down the channel. Unable to take any corrective action, she was swept against the apron at the foot of the North Pier and remained fast, with seas breaking over her. The lookouts at the roundhouse had witnessed her difficulties, and the life-saving apparatus and the lifeboat were immediately called out. The life-saving crew were on the scene within minutes, and the thirteen man crew got ashore with the aid of ropes, though several suffered rib and hand injuries in the process. The *Loch Lomond* was too severely damaged to be refloated, and was broken up on site.

23 October 1952 *Strathelliot* A 46 211 Tons/1915

The *Strathelliot* was one of the many trawlers built before and during the First World War by Hall Russells for the Aberdeen Steam Trawling & Fishing Co. Ltd's Strath fleet. After naval service in both World Wars, the *Strathelliot* returned to fishing in 1946 under the ownership of David Wood and others, and in 1949 was owned by the Clova Fishing Co. Ltd. She was making for shelter from a severe gale when she ran ashore on the Taing of Selwick in Hoy Sound at the western entrance to Scapa Flow. Stromness lifeboat immediately went to

Loch Lomond – *The **Loch Lomond** (A 299) pounded by heavy seas alongside the North Pier at Aberdeen Harbour after being dashed against the Pier while leaving harbour on 23 October 1952. Her 13-man crew were quickly rescued, but the **Loch Lomond** had to be broken up where she lay. (Photo Aberdeen Museum).*

'After the storm' – *Some of the crew of the* **Strathelliot** *preparing to salvage as much of the fishing gear as possible after their ship was stranded near Stromness on 23 October 1952. The ship herself became a total loss. (Photo George Coull Collection).*

Sunlight – *The* **Sunlight** *(A 221) aground on the rocks at the Spur of Murkle, on the shores of the Pentland Firth, shortly after the rescue of her crew by Thurso Lifeboat on 15 January 1953. (Photo George Coull Collection).*

her assistance but a first attempt to get alongside was frustrated by the severe weather. The lifeboat returned to Stromness to collect a life-saving crew with rockets, before returning to the scene to rescue all twelve crewmen, including Skipper George Simpson, 25 Grampian Road.

15 January 1953   *Sunlight*   A 221   203 Tons/1918

The *Sunlight* had been completed by Scotts of Bowling as the Admiralty Strath-class trawler *Thomas Graham*. She was loaned to the U.S. Navy in 1919, presumably for clearance of the Northern Mine Barrage. Sold in 1921, she passed to Grimsby owners, then in 1927 to North Shields owners who re-named her *Tynemouth Abbey*. She came to Aberdeen in December 1932 under the ownership of the Harrow-Baxter Steam Fishing Co. Ltd. who re-named her *Sunlight* in July 1933. Her second spell of war service began in July 1940 with her conversion to become a boom defence vessel, in which capacity she was engaged till July 1944. She was on her way to the northern fishing grounds when she ran ashore on the Spur of Murkle, five miles east of Thurso. In response to her radio distress signal and flares, Thurso lifeboat was launched to go to her aid and the Grimsby trawler *Loch Park* (formerly the Aberdeen trawler *Obsidian* (A 301)) stood by but was unable to close the stricken *Sunlight*. When the lifeboat arrived, the *Sunlight's* lee rail was under water, but in spite of the rough seas and the haze which covered the area, the lifeboat, under Coxswain McIntosh succeeded in getting alongside the *Sunlight* and taking off her crew of eleven:-

Skipper: Alex Souter, 22 Sutherland St. Buckie.
Mate: Robert Mitchell, 10 Hanover Street.
Chief Engineer: Peter Cooper, 47 Gilcomston Place.
Sec. Engineer: Alex Main, 7 Admiralty St. Portknockie.
Sec. Fisherman: J. Sutherland, 14 Hendry Terrace, Buckie.
Deckhand: G. Ritchie, 68 Wales Street.
Deckhand: A. Johnson, 51 Bedford Avenue.
Deckhand: H. Hay, 12 Castle St, Peterhead.
Fireman: A. Farquhar, c/o Hazlehead Nurseries.

Fireman: S. Murray, c/o Seamen's Mission.
Cook: A. Porter, 14 Logie Place.

Shortly after the rescue of the crew, the *Sunlight* slipped from the ledge on which she had grounded and fell on to her side, becoming a total loss.

27 March 1953   *River Lossie*   A 332   201 Tons/1920

The *River Lossie* was built by Fleming & Ferguson of Paisley as the Strath-class Admiralty trawler *Arthur Herwin*, but was too late for naval use. With twenty other ex-Admiralty trawlers, she was bought by the Montrose Fishing Co. Ltd. in 1920, registered as ME 121 and re-named *River Lossie*. She passed to Grimsby owners Consolidated Fisheries Ltd. and took the number GY 279 in 1923. She came to Aberdeen in 1935 under the ownership of Skipper J.K. Robertson. The *River Lossie* had the doubtful distinction of being one of the first Aberdeen trawlers to come under air attack, being targeted by a German bomber while fishing off Buchan Ness on the 7th December 1939, fortunately without damage. She was also instrumental in rescuing the crew of forty-one of the Newcastle steamer *Cairnmona* after she had been torpedoed by U-13 off Rattray Head on 30th October 1939. She was taken up for naval service as an armed patrol vessel in June 1940 and served till February 1945. At the time of her loss she was making for the shelter of Lerwick harbour when she grounded on Robbie Ramsay's Baa at the north entrance to the harbour. Lerwick lifeboat was soon in attendance but the crew remained aboard in the hope that their ship could be re-floated. By the following day, however, the *River Lossie* was half-full of water, so she was abandoned by her crew of eleven, under Skipper Alex Clark of Buckie, and became a total loss.

11 February 1954   *Koorah*   A 18   227 Tons/1912

The *Koorah* was registered in no less than five ports during her long life, but retained her original name throughout. Built by Hall Russell for Milford owners, she first carried the registration M 120 before being taken up

River Lossie – The **River Lossie**, later A 332, pictured while registered in Grimsby, fishing under the crown and colours of Consolidated Fisheries Ltd. She was lost at the north entrance to Lerwick Harbour on 27 March 1953. (Photo George Coull Collection).

River Lossie – The wreck of the **River Lossie** (A 332) as she lies on her side after running aground on Robbie Ramsay's Baa at the north entrance to Lerwick Harbour on 27 March 1953. (Photo Ian Hughson Lerwick).

Koorah – Built by Hall, Russells in 1912 for Milford haven owners, the **Koorah** distinguished herself at the Dardanelles compaign and during her career was registered at five different ports. She was lost near Dunnet Head, Caithness on 11 February 1954. (Photo George Coull Collection).

Doonie Braes – The **Doonie Braes** (A 881) ashore beneath the beetling cliffs near the Old Man of Hoy after running aground there on 20 April 1955. Her crew of twelve got safely away in their own boat. (Photo George Coull Collection).

for minesweeping in August 1914. By March 1915 she was heavily involved in the minesweeping effort for the Dardanelles campaign and distinguished herself by saving, under circumstances of great gallantry, the crew of the minesweeping trawler *Manx Hero*, which had been sunk in the Kephez minefield. Returned to fishing in 1919, she transferred to Grimsby owners registered as GY 122, before going to Granton in 1935 as GN 14. She was first registered in Aberdeen as A 249 in 1941 under the joint ownership of the Walker & Regent Fishing Companies, and was sold in 1944 to A. & M. Smith Ltd. of Hull, becoming H 77. In 1946 she returned to Aberdeen under the ownership of the Brebner Fishing Co. Ltd. and took the number A 18.

On what proved to be her last trip, she had been fishing off Strathy Point on the North Coast of Scotland, and was sheltering in the early morning in the lee of Dunnet Head awaiting daylight when she ran ashore on a reef of rocks half a mile west of Dunnet Head. In addition to firing distress rockets, a radio message was broadcast by Skipper James Findlay, and this was relayed to shore by the *Jean Stephen* (A 420), which was sheltering nearby in Thurso Bay. The *Jean Stephen* herself was lost in similar circumstances four years later, when she ran ashore in Sinclair Bay, not far from the present incident. The twelve-man crew had some difficulty in getting their smallboat into the water, with the result that when the crew got into it they found it to be leaking copiously and they had to bale continuously until they were able to board the Thurso seine-netter *Our Lassie*, which brought them to Scrabster. Later in the day the *Our Lassie* brought the skipper and mate back to the *Koorah*, and after their inspection the remainder of the crew were brought to the ship to prepare for a salvage attempt. Despite the efforts of a salvage tug, however, it was impossible to move the *Koorah*. Her crew were:-

Skipper: James Findlay, 41 Viewfield Road.
Mate: Lionel Lawrence, 11 Ashgrove Gdns South.
Chief Engineer: F. Mair, 4 Hayton Road.
Sec. Engineer: D. Guyan, 68 Wales Street.

Sec. Fisherman: J. Conway, 1 Kintore Place.
Deckhand: W. Donald, 74 Park Street.
Deckhand: J.C. Ewing, 27 Logie Avenue.
Deckhand: E. Walton, 13 Blackfriars Street.
Deckhand: D. Ewing, 57 Cove Bay.
Deckhand: J. Hepburn, 68 Garthdee Road.
Deckhand/Trimmer: P. Beattie, 29 Briarfield Terrace.
Cook: T.W. Brewster, 8 St. Clement Street.

20 April 1955   *Doonie Braes*   A 881   213 Tons/1918

The *Doonie Braes* was completed by Alexander Hall & Co. Ltd. as the Strath-class Admiralty trawler *George Coulston*. Sold by the Admiralty in 1922, she had a brief spell of Glasgow registration as GW 38 before being registered in Aberdeen under the ownership of Miss H.W. Lewis, and was re-named *Doonie Braes* in July 1922. Two other ex-Admiralty trawlers under the ownership of female members of the Lewis family were re-named *Bervie Braes* and *Boyne Braes* at the same time. The *Doonie Braes* seems to have been employed only as a steam liner, and was in the Navy as a danlayer and minesweeper from 1940 to 1945. She was one of the few steam liners still fishing when, on her way home from northern waters with a valuable catch including 135 cwts of line halibut, she ran ashore in thick mist hard against the cliffs, 120 yards north of the Old Man of Hoy, on Orkney's west coast. A Scapa-based naval M.F.V. spotted the trawler's distress flares, and approached close enough for the *Doonie Braes'* crew to row across in their smallboat and be taken to Lyness. Stromness lifeboat had been launched in answer to the distress call, and proceeded to the North Shoal, which was the position given by Skipper Robert Bruce of the *Doonie Braes*, and which was some ten miles north of the actual grounding. By the time the lifeboat located the *Doonie Braes*, her crew had been picked up by the M.F.V. The lifeboat later in the day brought Skipper Bruce and some of his crew back to the *Doonie Braes*, accompanied by the Orkney steamer *Orcadia*, in the hope that the *Doonie Braes* could be towed off, but she was found to be full of water and impossible to salvage.

19 October 1955 *Sturdee* **A 219   202 Tons/1919**

Completed by Hall Russells as the Strath-class Admiralty trawler *Michael Brian* too late for naval service, the *Sturdee* was re-named after being sold in 1919 to Hull and later Lowestoft owners (LT 988). She came to Aberdeen in 1932 under the ownership of Gore & Spence (later Gorspen Steam Trawling Co. Ltd.), and was later sold to A.A. Davidson in 1937 and to the Looker Fishing Co. Ltd. in 1946. She saw brief naval service from November 1939 to January 1940. At the time of her loss she was returning from an eight-day fishing trip when she went ashore in foggy conditions 150 yards off Aberdeen beach just north of the Beach Ballroom. The Bridge of Don life-saving apparatus crew were soon on the scene and fired a line over the trawler's deck. Just then, however, Aberdeen lifeboat under Coxswain George Flett arrived and succeeded in taking off all eleven of the crew, in spite of heavy seas which made rescue difficult. The *Sturdee*'s catch of fish was landed next day but the ship herself was a total loss, and she was broken up where she lay. The crew were:-

Skipper: William Wilson, Moray House, Macduff.
Mate: R. Rae, 3 Corndavon Terrace.
Chief Engineer: John A. Reid, 24 Anton St., Buckie.
Sec. Engineer, James Connell, 432 Hilton Drive.
Sec. Fisherman: Charles Trowbridge, 195 Victoria Road.
Deckhand: Larry McElhatton, 18 Brebner Crescent.
Deckhand: James Findlay, 6 Lemon Street.
Deckhand: John Morrice, 4 Cruden Park.
Cook: Gordon Westland, 19 Kincorth Avenue.
Fireman: Charles Shand, 21 Logie Avenue.
Fireman: William Watt, 7 Tullos Place.

Crewman James Findlay was to be a member of the crew of the *George Robb* (A 406) when she was lost with all hands in December 1959.

11 December 1956 *Northman* **A 652   199 Tons/1911**

Built by Hall Russells for the Standard Fishing Co. Ltd. the *Northman* was on only her third trip when she was in collision off Rattray Head with the Iceland trawler *Lord Nelson*, as the result of which the *Lord Nelson* sank, her crew being picked up by an accompanying vessel. The *Northman* was one of the first Aberdeen trawlers to be taken up for minesweeping in August 1914, continuing in this capacity till 1919, when she resumed her fishing career. Rather surprisingly, in view of her years, she was again taken up for naval service in July 1940 and fitted for anti-submarine duties; for at least a considerable part of her second naval career she was based in the Faroe Islands, along with the *Buchans II* (A 162) which had been fitted for similar duties, and was employed on convoy escort and guardship work. After her release in March 1946 she passed into the ownership of the Stephen Fishing Co. Ltd. On 5th February 1948, while on the last leg of a trip from the Faroe fishing grounds and in stormy conditions with a strong south-south-easterly wind, the *Northman* ran ashore on the Belhelvie sands about 8 pm. The twelve-man crew burned flares to attract attention. The Belhelvie life-saving brigade were soon on the scene and the Aberdeen lifeboat arrived before 10 pm. While endeavouring to get alongside the *Northman*, the lifeboat, under Coxswain Tom Sinclair, herself took the ground, and the twelve men were safely brought ashore by breeches buoy just as the Newburgh lifeboat was being hauled southwards on its carriage. The Aberdeen lifeboat was fast on the sands until the early hours of 9th February, when the hard-working crew, with the assistance of Aberdeen's No. 2 lifeboat and the local tug *St. Fotin*, succeeded in refloating her and bringing her to Aberdeen under her own power. The *Northman* herself remained stuck fast on the sands and was given up as a constructive total loss, her registration of A 414 being cancelled on 30th March 1948. She was, however, refloated later in the year and extensively refitted, including the addition of a whaleback by A.J. & R. Mitchell, Engineers, Peterhead, who re-registered the *Northman* in February 1950, taking the new registration A 652. She left Aberdeen in the early afternoon of 11th December 1956 for a fishing trip to Shetland waters and

Northman – The **Northman** (A 652) passing Hall Russell's Shipyard and the Floating Dock on her way to sea. She was wrecked on Keith Inch, Peterhead on 11 December 1956. Her crew of 13 were rescued by Peterhead Lifeboat. (Photo George Coull Collection).

Robert Limbrick – The **Robert Limbrick** was lost on the Island of Mull on 5 February 1957 with her crew of 12. She is photographed in Aberdeen in the early 1950's as the Walker Company's **Star of Freedom**. She was one of the Round Table class of minesweepers built in 1942 from plans of the Company's **Star of Orkney** of 1936. (Photo George Coull Collection).

Carency – The **Carency** (A 129) on the rocks near Noss Head, Wick, while preparations are made to tow her off. Wick Lifeboat is alongside her. She sank shortly after being towed from the rocks by the **Gilmar** (A 300) on 28 June 1957. (Photo George Coull Collection).

Jean Stephen – The **Jean Stephen** (A 420) setting out on a fishing trip from Aberdeen Harbour. Her fireman is obviously busy in the stokehold. The **Jean Stephen** was stranded at Sinclair Bay, Caithness, on 18 January 1958. (Photo Courtesy Robert Wiseman).

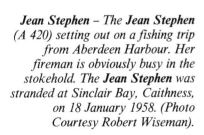

struck the rocks at the South Head off Keith Inch, Peterhead, only 400 yards from the engineering works of her owners, with such a crash that the impact was heard over much of Peterhead. Peterhead lifeboat, under coxswain James Strachan, was launched in answer to the blasts on the trawler's siren, and was twice dashed against the *Northman's* side by the heavy swell before successfully rescuing the thirteen-man crew in twos and threes. The crew were:-

Skipper: Edward J. Slater (41), 23 Balmoral Road.
Mate: John Campbell (42), 7 North Blantyre Street, Findochty.
Chief Engineer: John Howie (41), 6 Gillanhill Place, Mastrick.
Sec. Engineer: Stephen Knox (29), 47 Fernhill Road, Mastrick.
Sec. Fisherman: Alex M. Davidson (41), 9 Moir Green, Rosehill.
Deckhand: Douglas Cowie (26), 18 Main Street, Buckie.
Deckhand: David Ferrier (53), 14 Queen St. Gourdon.
Deckhand: George F. Garden (21), 10 Gadle Braes, Peterhead.
Deckhand: Thomas O'Rourke (26), 12 Uphill Lane, Peterhead.
Deckhand: Patrick O'Connell (25), Deepsea Mission, Aberdeen.
Cook: George Morrice (52), 533 North Anderson Drive.
Fireman: George Petrie (53), 16 Marchburn Avenue.
Fireman: William Groves (40), 8 Castlehill Barracks.

5 February 1957   *Robert Limbrick*   A 283

273 Tons/1942

Although she had never sailed from Aberdeen under that name, the *Robert Limbrick* had been built by Hall Russells as the Round Table-class Admiralty trawler *Sir Galahad*. All eight ships of the class were built in Aberdeen, four each by Hall Russells and John Lewis Ltd. and were named after the knights of King Arthur's Round Table. They were designed to be easily converted to commercial use when their naval duties were over, and

Sir Galahad was bought by the Walker Steam Trawling & Fishing Co. Ltd. in February 1947 and re-named *Star of Freedom*. In March 1956 she was sold to Milford Fisheries Ltd, who re-named her *Robert Limbrick*, retaining her Aberdeen registration. While on her way to the fishing grounds with a twelve-man Milford crew, the *Robert Limbrick* ran ashore on rocks at Quinish Point, seven miles from Ardmore on the Isle of Mull. No distress signals had been heard, and the wreck was discovered by a Fraserburgh drifter. There were no survivors.

28 June 1957   *Carency*   A 129   233 Tons/1916

Soon after completion for Grimsby owners at the yard of Cook, Welton & Gemmell Ltd. at Beverley, the *Carency* was taken over by the Navy and served as a minesweeper till 1919. She was again taken over by the Navy in 1940, for use as an anti-submarine and examination vessel. On her release in June 1946 she was purchased by William and John Wood of Aberdeen and passed into the ownership of William Wood & Sons in 1949. Under Skipper David Wood, 72 Louisville Avenue, one of the owners, the *Carency* ran ashore in thick fog at Greenigoe, one mile north of Wick. The Wick life-saving apparatus and Wick lifeboat, under Coxswain Neil Stewart were soon on the scene, and the life-saving apparatus crew put a line to the trawler soon after their arrival. Skipper Wood was confident that his ship could be salvaged, however, and retained his twelve-man crew on board until the arrival of the trawler *Gilmar* (A 300), also owned by William Wood & Sons. Wick lifeboat, which had been standing by for fourteen hours, took off the crew and transferred Skipper Wood to the *Gilmar*, which succeeded in moving the stranded *Carency* about twenty feet before she stuck fast again. Two hours later, the *Carency* rolled from the rocks and sank.

18 January 1958   *Jean Stephen*   A 420   212 Tons/1917

The *Jean Stephen* had been built by Alexander Hall & Co. Ltd. as the *Savitri* (GY 1028), and was taken up immediately for minelaying and later minesweeping duties. She was released by the Navy in 1919, and was sold to Granton owners in 1928, taking the number GN 9. She was purchased in October 1936 and immediately re-named by the Stephen Fishing Co. Ltd. of Aberdeen. At the time of her loss, the *Jean Stephen* had been sheltering in Sinclair Bay, to the north of Wick, with several other trawlers. Skipper John Cowie, 119 Grampian Road, was in the process of getting under way for the fishing grounds when a blizzard struck and the *Jean Stephen* was driven on to the beach. A radio fault prevented Skipper Cowie from contacting Wick Radio, but the Aberdeen trawler *Strathdee* relayed the distress call and Wick lifeboat and life-saving apparatus were soon in attendance. The lifeboat stood by for several hours before the crew came ashore by breeches buoy.

9 December 1958   *George H. Hastie*   A 27
229 Tons/1916

Another Hall-built ship, the *George H. Hastie* (SN 274), was completed for the North Shields family firm of R. Hastie & Sons Ltd. who operated most of their ships from Aberdeen. She was taken up for minesweeping until 1918. After many years fishing out of Aberdeen with her North Shields registration, she was sold in 1957 to North Eastern Fisheries Ltd. who registered her in Aberdeen as A 27. As with most of her steam-driven contemporaries, age had caught up with the *George H. Hastie*, and she was on her delivery voyage to Germany for breaking up when she ran aground on the Island of Amrum. Her passage crew of seven got safely away in their liferaft.

4 February 1959   *Strathcoe*   A 6   215 Tons/1916

The *Strathcoe* was another trawler with a rather unusual life. She was built by Hall Russells during World War 1 for the Strath fleet of the Aberdeen Steam Trawling & Fishing Co. Ltd. and was immediately taken up for minelaying and later minesweeping work. She was purchased by the Admiralty in August 1918, and was retained in the Navy until after World War II, being the only trawler to have this distinction. After "demob" in 1946, she was bought by Granton owners and registered as GN 21, before being bought by Bruces Stores (Aberdeen) Ltd. in February 1955 and taking the registration A 6. Under Skipper James Herd, 14 Upper Mastrick Way, the *Strathcoe* was making for Aberdeen with 250 boxes of fish after a nine-day fishing trip to West coast waters when, at 2.30 am in gale-force winds, she ran ashore beneath precipitous 550-feet cliffs two miles south of Rackwick Head in the Orkney Isles. It was much too dangerous to launch the liferaft, so Skipper Herd fired off two distress flares and radioed for Longhope lifeboat, which arrived within an hour of the trawler going aground, but had to wait for the tide to start ebbing before attempting a rescue. Meanwhile the shipwrecked crew had crowded into the trawler's wheelhouse to seek shelter from the mountainous waves which were pounding their ship. At 5.18 am the lifeboat made contact with the *Strathcoe* by breeches buoy, and the first man to leave the ship was the oldest member of the crew — 60-year-old Alexander Buchan, 96 Provost Fraser Drive. On his way across to the lifeboat, however, he was swept out of the breeches buoy by the heavy seas but managed to save himself by holding on to the rope of the buoy and hauling himself hand over hand to the lifeboat. The lifeboat Coxswain now deemed it too dangerous to try to rescue the remaining thirteen men by breeches buoy, and had repeatedly to work the lifeboat alongside the *Strathcoe* to enable the crew to jump aboard, before bringing the whole fourteen-man crew to Longhope. The youngest crew member was fifteen-year-old Gordon Duff, 3 Manor Walk, who told reporters "This won't stop me going back to sea. I'm going back again as soon as possible." The other crew members were:-

Mate: George Mutch, 54a Victoria Road.
Sec. Fisherman: George Cusiter, 18 Upper Mastrick Way.
  Alistair Muirhead, 120 Willowpark Crescent.
  Frederick Winter, 5 Ferrier Crescent.
  Alan Scott, 32 Ruthrie Road.
  John McLean, 47 Kirkhill Road.

*River Ayr – The **River Ayr** (A 337) enters Aberdeen Harbour at the end of a fishing trip. The absence of trawl gallows and winch indicates that she was working as a line-fishing vessel and the 'quarantine' flag flying above her wheelhouse shows that she had visited some foreign port, probably Faroe, where much line-fishing was done. The **River Ayr** was later fitted for trawling and foundered off Shetland on 16 April 1959. (Photo George Coull Collection).*

Alexander Leslie, 7 Ferrier Gardens.
Thomas Robinson, 170 Crown Street.
Alan Stewart, 41 Heathryfold Circle.
George Wood, 22 Constitution Street.
David Cowie, 23 Seatown, Buckie.

16 April 1959   *River Ayr*   A 337   202 Tons/1917

The *River Ayr* had been built by the Montrose Shipbuilding Co. Ltd. for the Admiralty as the Strath-class minesweeping trawler *Charles Carroll*. Sold in 1919, she was re-named *River Ayr* (ME 79), owned by the Montrose Fishing Co. Ltd., later being registered in London before being bought in 1923 by Consolidated Fisheries Ltd. of Grimsby and registered as GY 278. She came to Aberdeen in 1935 under the ownership of H. Gore, and subsequently changed ownership on several occasions. At the time of her loss she sprang a leak sixteen miles south-east of the Bard Head, Bressay, Shetland and

was taken in tow by the Aberdeen trawler *Kosmos* (A 712). Her pumps could not cope with the leak, however, and she foundered before she could she got to the safety of Lerwick harbour. By a strange coincidence, the *Kosmos* had towed the *River Ayr* to Aberdeen in in November 1957 when the *River Ayr* suffered a steering failure.

6 December 1959   *George Robb*   A 406
217 Tons/1930

The *George Robb* was built by Hall Russells for Newhaven owner Robert Carnie as the *Elise I. Carnie* and registered in Granton GN 24. She was bought by George Robb & Sons Ltd. in 1936, re-named *George Robb* and registered in Aberdeen (A 406). She was taken up by the Navy on 30th August 1939 and served as a minesweeper until her release in February 1946. In 1959, when almost all of Aberdeen's fleet of steam trawlers had already gone for scrapping, it was felt that the *George Robb*, at less than thirty years old, had some years of life left in her sturdy hull, and she was therefore taken in hand for conversion to diesel power, the work being completed at Lowestoft in October 1959. On her return to Aberdeen she completed one trip successfully before setting out at 11.30 am on a Sunday morning for what was to prove to be her last trip. Almost exactly twelve hours later, Caithness farmer William Ham and his wife had just driven home to their farm at Mey, eight miles west of Duncansby Head after a visit to Mrs. Ham's father at Duncansby. Outside, the wind had got up to storm force. As was his custom before bed-time, Mr. Ham switched on his trawler-band radio just in time to hear, at 11.50 pm, the message "Ashore south of Duncansby. Making water rapidly. Require immediate assistance." Mr. and Mrs. Ham got back into their car, drove back to Duncansby to collect Mrs. Ham's father, brother, sister and a neighbour, before setting off with torches to search along the treacherous cliffs.

After walking for about a mile in conditions so wild that it was difficult to keep on their feet, they heard the sound of the trawler's siren and then saw that the trawler was lying among rocks near the dreaded Stacks of Duncansby, huge fangs of rocks below the cliffs. They thought the men had seen the lights of their torches as the siren was sounded once or twice more before becoming silent. The six made their way back to Duncansby Head Lighthouse, where life-saving teams from Wick and Scarfskerry were already gathering, and led them to where they had found the *George Robb*. There was no sign of life on board, the ship was being battered ceaselessly by huge waves, and it was obvious that, even if the life-saving teams were to succeed in getting a line to the trawler, it would be impossible for anyone on board to recover it and make it fast. The Longhope lifeboat could be seen standing off the shore, but she was powerless to render any assistance. Several people succeeded in making their way down the cliffs and commenced a search for survivors. One body was found

and taken up the cliffs, but there was no sign of survivors. One of the life-saving brigade, Station Officer Eric Campbell, of Wick, collapsed and died in the atrocious conditions.

Twelve men died on that fearsome night, leaving nine widows and thirty-four fatherless children. Skipper Marshall Ryles was on only his second trip on the *George Robb*. The crew were:-

Skipper: Marshall Ryles (31), 525 North Anderson Drive. (Widow and four children).
Mate: Peter Dempster (24), 56 Alexander Drive, Hayton (Married only four months).
Sec. Fisherman: Bruno Saborowski (39), 62 Crombie Road, (ex-Polish army — single).
Chief Engineer: William McKay (35), 67 Strathmore Drive, Mastrick (Widow and three children).
Sec. Engineer: Robert Dugan (38), 41 Arbroath Way, Kincorth. (Widow and three children).
Third Engineer: William Farquhar (47), 1 Slater Crescent, Portknockie. (Widow and three children).
Cook: William Duthie (47), 4 Beacon Cotts, Cairnbulg. (Widow and seven family — three at school).
Deckhand: James Findlay (30), 47 Davidson Place, Mastrick. (Widow and four children). (Survivor of the *Sturdee* lost on 19th October 1955).
Deckhand: James Adams (45), 54 Marchburn Crescent, Northfield. (Widow and six family).
Deckhand: David Lockhart, 72 Grampian Place.
Deckhand: Albert Smith· (45), 41 Alexander Drive, Hayton. (Widow and four children).
Deckhand: George Duffy (25), 42 Menzies Road.

13 June 1961   *D.W. Fitzgerald*   A 629   235 Tons/1916

Built by Hall Russell for Richard Irvin and Sons Ltd. the *D.W. Fitzgerald* was immediately taken up for minesweeping and retained by the Navy till 1919. She was again taken up for minesweeping from August 1940 till December 1945. She was one of the last of Aberdeen's steam trawlers when she was sold for scrapping, and was being towed to the scrapyard by the *Cadorna* (A 125). She

George Robb – The **George Robb** *(A 406) before her conversion to diesel power. (Photo George Coull Collection).*

George Robb – The *George Robb* (A 406) after conversion from steam to diesel. She had completed only one trip in her new form before she was lost on 6 December 1959, one mile from Duncansby Head Lighthouse. (Photo George Coull Collection).

George Robb – The *George Robb* (A 406) lies broken on the jagged rocks near Duncansby Head Lighthouse after being driven ashore in a severe storm on 6 December 1959. All twelve members of her crew were lost. (Photo George Coull Collection).

was unmanned and was lashed alongside the *Cadorna* by chains. As the two ships reached the harbour bar outside the entrance channel of Aberdeen harbour, the motion of the ships in the swell burst the chains and the *D.W. Fitzgerald* was driven ashore by the tide beneath Girdleness Lighthouse, at the same place as the *Ben Screel* had been wrecked in 1933. It was found impossible to refloat her and she was in the process of being broken up on site when she rolled from her rocky perch one night and sank. Fortunately, no-one was on board at the time.

*D.W. Fitzgerald – The **D.W. Fitzgerald** (A 629) in a sad state of dereliction beneath the lighthouse at Girdleness, Aberdeen. She rolled over and sank before scrapping could be completed. (Photo Courtesy Angus MacLeod).*

ABERDEEN STEAM TRAWLER LOSSES

INDEX

Name of Vessel	Reg. No.	Date of Loss	Name of Vessel	Reg. No.	Date of Loss
Aberdeenshire	A 234	21 October 1910	*Ben Strome*	A 109	27 July 1941
Active (1)	A 776	26 April 1917	*Ben Torc*	A 604	6 September 1927
Active (2)	A 897	18 December 1939	*Ben Venue*	A 83	6 April 1904
Amadavat	A 619	10 December 1917	*Ben Wyvis*	A 301	4 December 1908
Ant	A 308	25 September 1916	*Bonito*	A 93	20 December 1894
Argo	A 196	30 April 1917	*Braconash*	A 728	29 April 1932
Arora	A 320	23 January 1941	*Braconburn*	A 768	30 July 1944
Aster	A 762	13 October 1917	*Braconbush*	A 770	29 January 1942
Avondon	A 136	22 December 1936	*Braconhill*	A 904	9 January 1913
Avondow	A 56	27 February 1933	*Braconlea*	A 227	5 October 1952
Avonglen	A 137	19 September 1934	*Braconmoor (1)*	A 164	15 January 1916
Badger	A 877	26 May 1906	*Braconmoor (2)*	A 767	5 January 1930
Balmedie	A 113	27 April 1915	*Bravo*	A 305	24 January 1927
Banffshire	A 349	16 January 1905	*Breadalbane*	A 281	30 November 1920
Bass Rock	A 759	24 September 1940	*Briton*	A 101	21 July 1915
Beathwood	A 442	11 September 1940	*Caersin*	A 427	28 November 1926
Belcher	A 341	4 September 1903	*Campania (1)*	A 486	9 February 1904
Belmont	A 101	26 January 1928	*Campania (2)*	A 437	26 June 1915
Ben Ardna (1)	A 517	8 August 1915	*Carency*	A 129	28 June 1957
Ben Ardna (2)	A 417	12 May 1942	*Cassandra*	A 236	26 August 1935
Ben Dearg	A 566	9 September 1908	*Cepheus*	A 656	9 March 1920
Ben Doran	A 178	29 March 1930	*Chancellor*	A 206	29 March 1936
Ben Gairn	A 738	4 May 1941	*Chinkiang*	A 798	12 April 1917
Ben Heilem	A 470	8 October 1917	*Choice*	A 764	27 August 1931
Benington	A 236	7 May 1915	*Christabelle*	A 360	26 February 1941
Ben Lawers	A 311	30 April 1930	*Chrysoprasus*	A 145	3 June 1915
Ben More	A 82	23 December 1911	*City of York*	A 324	15 October 1939
Ben Namur	A 244	10 October 1920	*Clan Gordon*	A 902	1 April 1911
Ben Nevis	A 821	16 February 1900	*Clover Bank (1)*	A 379	24 April 1916
Ben Rinnes	A 488	27 March 1928	*Clover Bank (2)*	A 731	15 February 1918
Ben Roy	A 94	20 December 1909	*Commander*	A 226	24 June 1915
Ben Screel	A 121	18 January 1933	*Corena*	A 198	September 1948

Name of Vessel	Reg. No.	Date of Loss	Name of Vessel	Reg. No.	Date of Loss
Corennie	A 228	28 May 1940	*Empress*	A 289	23 December 1915
Cortes	A 290	4 June 1915	*Endeavour*	A 493	10 March 1918
Countess	A 642	22 January 1901	*Espera*	A 246	26 January 1937
Craigendarroch	A 51	31 July 1924	*Ethel Crawford*	A 36	20 April 1945
Craig Gowan	A 779	12 November 1896	*Evelyn*	A 266	3 September 1936
Cransdale	A 453	21 January 1931	*Evening Star (1)*	A 530	4 June 1915
Crathie (1)	A 350	27 August 1914	*Evening Star (2)*	A 406	9 May 1927
Crathie (2)	A 713	16 December 1916	*Evergreen*	A 184	18 January 1936
Crimond	A 334	19 May 1915	*Explorer*	A 535	4 June 1915
Crisabelle Stephen	A 374	16 January 1939	*Fastnet*	A 422	9 April 1894
Crown Prince	A 369	12 April 1917	*Fernbank*	A 910	16 November 1941
Cruiser	A 882	November 1919	*Festing Grindall*	A 630	4 October 1928
Cruiser	GN 54	2 May 1915	*Fife Ness*	A 377	12 April 1917
Curlew	A 906	3 February 1922	*Flavia*	A 373	23 August 1940
D.W. Fitzgerald	A 629	13 June 1961	*Florence Dombey*	A 264	5 May 1933
Dandini	A 18	7 May 1938	*Gareloch*	A 276	18 August 1935
Danearn	A 395	15 March 1942	*George*	A 345	3 January 1911
Daneden	A 59	19 December 1939	*George Aunger*	A 37	25 April 1930
Danella	A 902	26 October 1936	*George H. Hastie*	A 27	9 December 1958
Davan	A 117	25 September 1931	*George Milburn*	A 634	12 July 1917
Deeside	A 397	21 January 1917	*George Robb*	A 406	6 December 1959
Delphine	A 126	20 November 1939	*George Stroud*	A 88	25 December 1935
Dewdrop	A 11	27 October 1899	*Gladwyn*	A 949	21 January 1928
Donside	A 155	7 January 1917	*Glenbervie*	A 364	15 October 1909
Doonie Braes	A 881	20 April 1955	*Glencarse*	A 605	18 April 1915
Drumblade	A 133	22 May 1924	*Glengairn*	A 203	23 March 1901
Drumoak	A 516	5 October 1914	*Glengarry*	A 207	5 October 1920
Drumtochty	A 408	29 January 1918	*Glenlossie*	A 205	25 May 1906
Duke of York	A 422	9 February 1917	*Glenshee*	A 386	5 October 1920
Eagle	A 874	28 September 1919	*Golden Sceptre*	A 115	19 January 1937
Ebenezer	A 892	4 June 1915	*Gorspen*	A 376	3 April 1940
Edith	A 780	8 July 1924	*Hood*	A 11	12 August 1938
Effort	A 487	22 October 1916	*Horace E. Nutten*	A 552	29 March 1941
Eileen Duncan	A 413	30 September 1941	*Ibis*	A 61	21 March 1904
Elizabeth Angela	A 322	13 August 1940	*Imperial Prince*	A 146	19 October 1923
Elswick	A 97	20 January 1942	*Jackdaw*	A ?	2 December 1915
Emperor	A 610	10 February 1926	*Jane Ross*	A 454	14 September 1934

Name of Vessel	Reg. No.	Date of Loss	Name of Vessel	Reg. No.	Date of Loss
Japonica	A 193	5 June 1915	*Lonicera*	A 91	19 December 1925
Jean Stephen	A 420	18 January 1958	*Lord Wimborne*	A 441	27 March 1943
Jessie Nutten	A 243	4 September 1916	*Lucerne*	SD	19 May 1915
Jessie Wetherly	A 228	5 April 1910	*Lucida*	A 175	11 January 1940
John E. Lewis	A 354	16 January 1918	*Maggie Ross*	A 449	4 April 1917
John G. Watson	A 327	31 October 1915	*Mansfield*	A 685	7 April 1934
John Nutten	A 846	11 April 1909	*Marec*	A 148	29 May 1907
Joseph Hodgkins	A 186	28 December 1921	*Margaret Clark*	A 1	10 December 1933
Kate	A 736	2 October 1905	*Margaret Stephen*	A 885	23 February 1936
Keith Hall	A 636	27 November 1921	*Martaban*	A 527	2 May 1915
Kilrenny	A 388	13 October 1911	*Mediator*	A 483	2 January 1916
Kinclaven	A 17	27 March 1941	*Merlin*	A 44	25 September 1909
Kincorth	A 263	10 December 1941	*Mirabelle*	A 176	17 September 1944
Kingfisher	A 613	1 April 1924	*Misten Braes*	A 362	25 January 1944
Knowsie	A 306	25 November 1910	*Mormond*	A 293	8 March 1910
Koorah	A 18	11 February 1954	*Morococala*	A 238	19 November 1917
Kuvera	A 384	26 January 1950	*Nairn*	A 524	2 December 1931
Lady Betty Balfour	A 864	8 October 1922	*New Dawn*	A 221	23 March 1918
Largo Bay	A 372	12 April 1917	*Nightingale*	A 556	22 April 1917
Lebanon	A 441	23 June 1915	*Nisus*	A 318	30 March 1941
Leith NB	A 389	21 December 1945	*North East*	A 473	20 December 1894
Lillian	A 603	12 April 1917	*Northman*	A 652	11 December 1956
Loch Ard (1)	A 503	10 September 1917	*North Sea*	A 245	17 November 1893
Loch Ard (2)	A 151	16 January 1934	*North West*	A 478	28 February 1918
Loch Assater	A 321	23 March 1940	*Ocean Queen*	A 175	6 August 1915
Loch Esk	A 241	12 May 1929	*Ocean Racer*	A 671	25 December 1902
Loch Eye	A 693	20 April 1917	*Ocean Scout 1*	A 362	21 December 1917
Loch Lomond	A 299	23 October 1952	*Ocean Victor*	A 7	5 August 1941
Loch Loyal	A 733	8 August 1940	*Oriole*	A 305	11 January 1941
Loch Morar	A 361	31 March 1937	*Orthos*	A 591	9 April 1917
Lochnagar	A 292	5 January 1909	*Osprey*	A 366	12 April 1917
Loch Naver	A 45	13 May 1918	*Palmerston*	A 328	8 April 1887
Loch Shiel	A 273	26 September 1916	*Peregrine*	A 895	23 April 1918
Loch Shin	A 78	28 May 1940	*Petrel*	A 515	4 June 1915
Loch Tay	A 888	21 March 1905	*Philorth*	A 376	6 December 1915
Loch Tummel	A 494	14 July 1918	*Pitstruan*	A 585	13 April 1917
Loch Wasdale	A 457	15 December 1942	*Plethos*	A 545	23 April 1918

Name of Vessel	Reg. No.	Date of Loss	Name of Vessel	Reg. No.	Date of Loss
Port Jackson	A 222	23 August 1935	*Star of the Sea*	A 538	21 January 1917
Premier	A 471	20 June 1915	*Star of the Wave*	A 913	10 January 1926
Prestige	A 793	6 November 1902	*Star of the West*	A 548	5 June 1915
Pretoria	A 941	5 February 1936	*Star of Victory*	A 4	24 October 1939
Procyon	A 899	17 November 1927	*Strathalford*	A 50	30 April
Quixotic	A 189	5 December 1939	*Strathalmond*	A 320	3 March 1913
Raindrop	A 434	6 July 1931	*Strathatholl*	A 477	15 March 1935
Ray	A 917	12 March 1920	*Strathbeg*	A 90	11 September 1907
Redcap	A 526	22 January 1906	*Strathborve*	A 139	6 September 1941
Renaissance	A 314	25 March 1928	*Strathbran (1)*	A 137	3 June 1915
River Ayr	A 337	16 April 1959	*Strathbran (2)*	A 536	5 October 1924
River Lossie	A 332	27 March 1953	*Strathclunie*	A 583	6 January 1928
River Ness	A 940	10 June 1940	*Strathcoe*	A 6	4 February 1959
Rob Roy	A 417	26 July 1912	*Strathelliot*	A 46	23 October 1952
Robert Limbrick	A 283	5 February 1957	*Stratherrick*	A 105	29 June 1939
Robert Smith	A 353	20 July 1917	*Strathgairn*	A 251	1 July 1941
Rochebonne	A 433	7 April 1941	*Strathgarry*	A 97	6 July 1915
Rodney	A 73	12 August 1912	*Strathlochy*	A 596	28 July 1941
Roslin (1)	A 8	24 July 1915	*Strathmoray*	A 480	17 April 1928
Roslin (2)	A 371	4 November 1937	*Strathmore*	A 136	24 July 1915
St. Andrew	A 670	24 December 1912	*Strathmiglo*	A 163	2 September 1932
St. Nicholas	A 489	4 November 1912	*Strathrannoch*	A 752	6 April 1917
Sanguine	A 359	20 July 1931	*Strathrye*	A 597	12 January 1941
Sansonnet	A 862	3 April 1940	*Strathtay*	A 661	9 February 1900
Sapphire	A 889	19 February 1919	*Strathurie*	A 403	28 June 1933
Schiehallion	A 905	9 June 1915	*Strathyre*	A 41	19 March 1912
Scottish Belle	A 512	4 September 1924	*Stromness*	A 380	4 October 1939
Scottish Queen	A 384	3 May 1915	*Struan*	A 718	18 January 1933
Sisters Melville	A 459	13 February 1917	*Sturdee*	A 219	19 October 1955
Skomer	A 194	15 May 1911	*Sunbeam*	A 680	31 October 1905
Soar	A 284	18 March 1940	*Sunlight*	A 221	15 January 1953
Star of Deveron	A 55	30 September 1941	*Sunray*	A 669	2 May 1915
Star of Learney	A 387	25 December 1942	*Suzette*	A 346	11 July 1941
Star of Peace	A 323	22 July 1915	*Swallow*	A 112	1 September 1905
Star of the East (1)	A 565	14 April 1905	*Taurus*	A 655	26 June 1917
Star of the East (2)	A 434	3 March 1946	*Teal*	A 428	1 June 1917
Star of the Isles	A 561	18 January 1907	*Tento*	A 90	6 February 1900

Name of Vessel	Reg. No.	Date of Loss
Thomas W. Irvin	A 421	27 August 1914
Toiler	A 50	31 March 1887
Tyne Wave	A 736	23 April 1918
Ulster	A 337	23 January 1925
Vale of Endrick	A 496	19 March 1914
Vale of Leven	A 177	10 July 1917
Venetia	A 560	2 January 1933
Viceroy	A 598	23 June 1915
Victory	A 692	6 March 1934
Vine	A 279	24 June 1915
Vineyard	A 787	8 November 1916
Welsh Prince	A 280	12 August 1916
William Butler	A 695	2 March 1928
William Morrison	A 355	28 November 1915
William Osten	A 856	26 October 1909
William Stephen	A 24	25 October 1943

BIBLIOGRAPHY

Aberdeen Free Press.

Aberdeen Daily Journal.

Aberdeen Press & Journal.

Aberdeen Evening Express.

Aberdeen Bon-Accord & Northern Pictorial.

Aberdeen Weekly Journal.

To the Rescue — J.L. Duthie, Aberdeen 1981.

The Lifeline — Norman Trewern, Aberdeen 1985.

Swept Channels — Taffrail, 1935.

The Auxiliary Patrol — E.K. Chatterton, 1923.

Warships of World War I — F.J. Dittmar & J.J. Colledge, 1972.

Warships of World War II — Lenton & Colledge, 1964.

British Merchant Shipping Losses World war I — H.M.S.O. 1919.

British Merchant Vessels Lost or Damaged by Enemy Action During World War II — H.M.S.O. 1947.

Marine News (Journal of the World Ship Society).

Lloyds Registers

The Fisherman's Nautical Almanack, Aberdeen.

Olsen's Fisherman's Nautical Almanack, Scarborough.